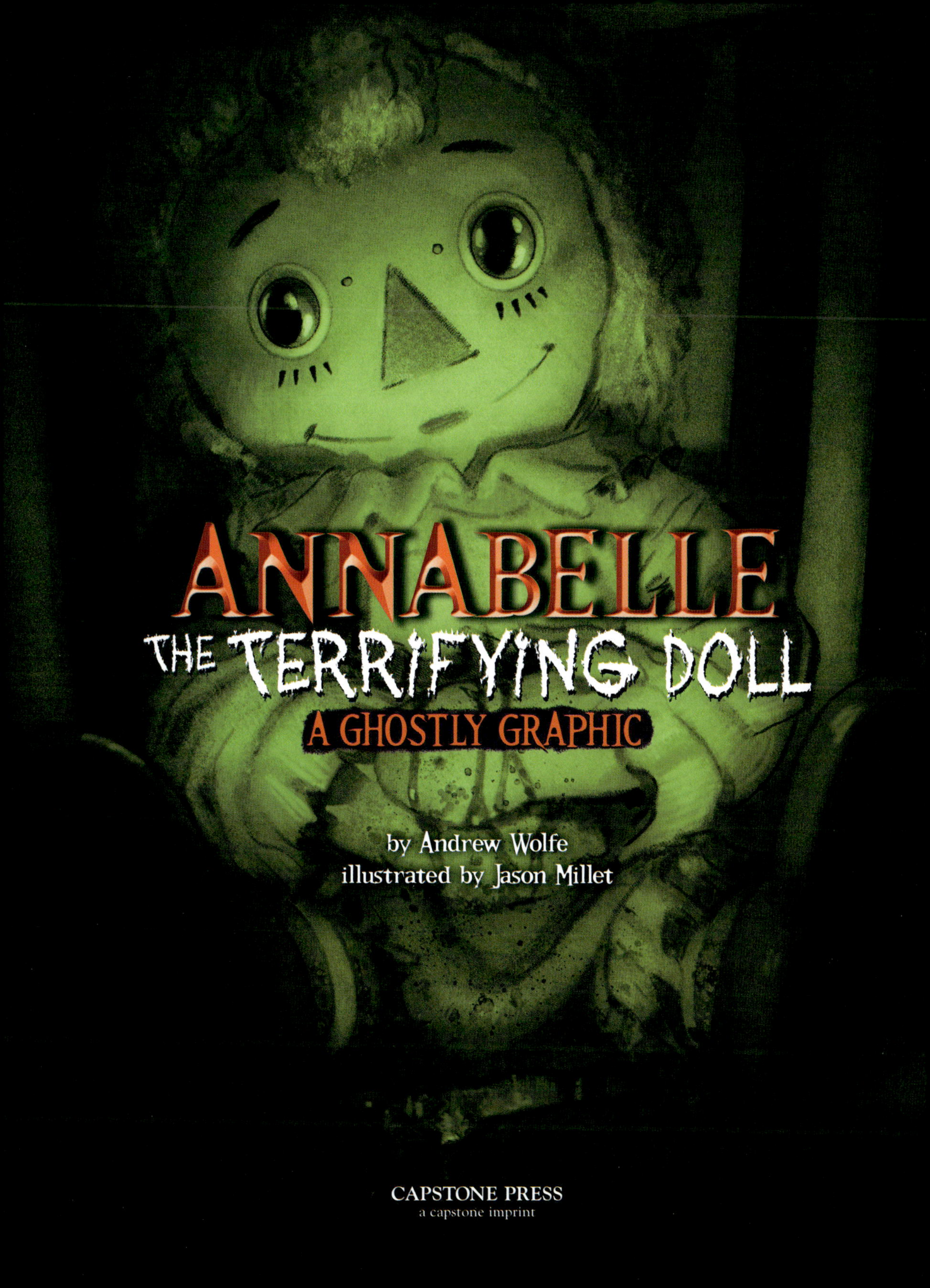

ANNABELLE
THE TERRIFYING DOLL
A GHOSTLY GRAPHIC

by Andrew Wolfe
illustrated by Jason Millet

CAPSTONE PRESS
a capstone imprint

Published by Capstone Press, an imprint of Capstone
1710 Roe Crest Drive, North Mankato, Minnesota 56003
capstonepub.com

Copyright © 2025 by Capstone. All rights reserved. No part of this publication may be reproduced in whole or in part, or stored in a retrieval system, or transmitted in any form or by any means, electronic, mechanical, photocopying, recording, or otherwise, without written permission of the publisher.

Library of Congress Cataloging-in-Publication Data
is available on the Library of Congress website.

ISBN: 9781669068440 (hardcover)
ISBN: 9781669071280 (paperback)
ISBN: 9781669068587 (ebook PDF)

Summary: In 1970, a nursing student was given a large doll as a gift. Soon, the doll—which became known as Annabelle—began acting strange. When no one was looking, Annabelle changed positions on her own. Then the doll began leaving creepy, cryptic notes asking for help. Was Annabelle possessed by the spirit of a dead girl? Or was the doll an anchor for a demon?

Editorial Credits
Editor: Christopher Harbo; Designer: Sarah Bennett;
Production Specialist: Katy LaVigne

Any additional websites and resources referenced in this book are not maintained, authorized, or sponsored by Capstone. All product and company names are trademarks™ or registered® trademarks of their respective holders.

TABLE OF CONTENTS

Introduction
THE PARANORMAL INVESTIGATORS 4

Chapter 1
THE NURSES 6

Chapter 2
THE GIRL IN THE FIELD 16

Chapter 3
THE ATTACK 22

Chapter 4
THE POSSESSION 30

Chapter 5
THE FINAL RESTING PLACE 36

MORE ABOUT ANNABELLE 44
GLOSSARY 46
READ MORE 47
INTERNET SITES 47
ABOUT THE AUTHOR 48
ABOUT THE ILLUSTRATOR 48

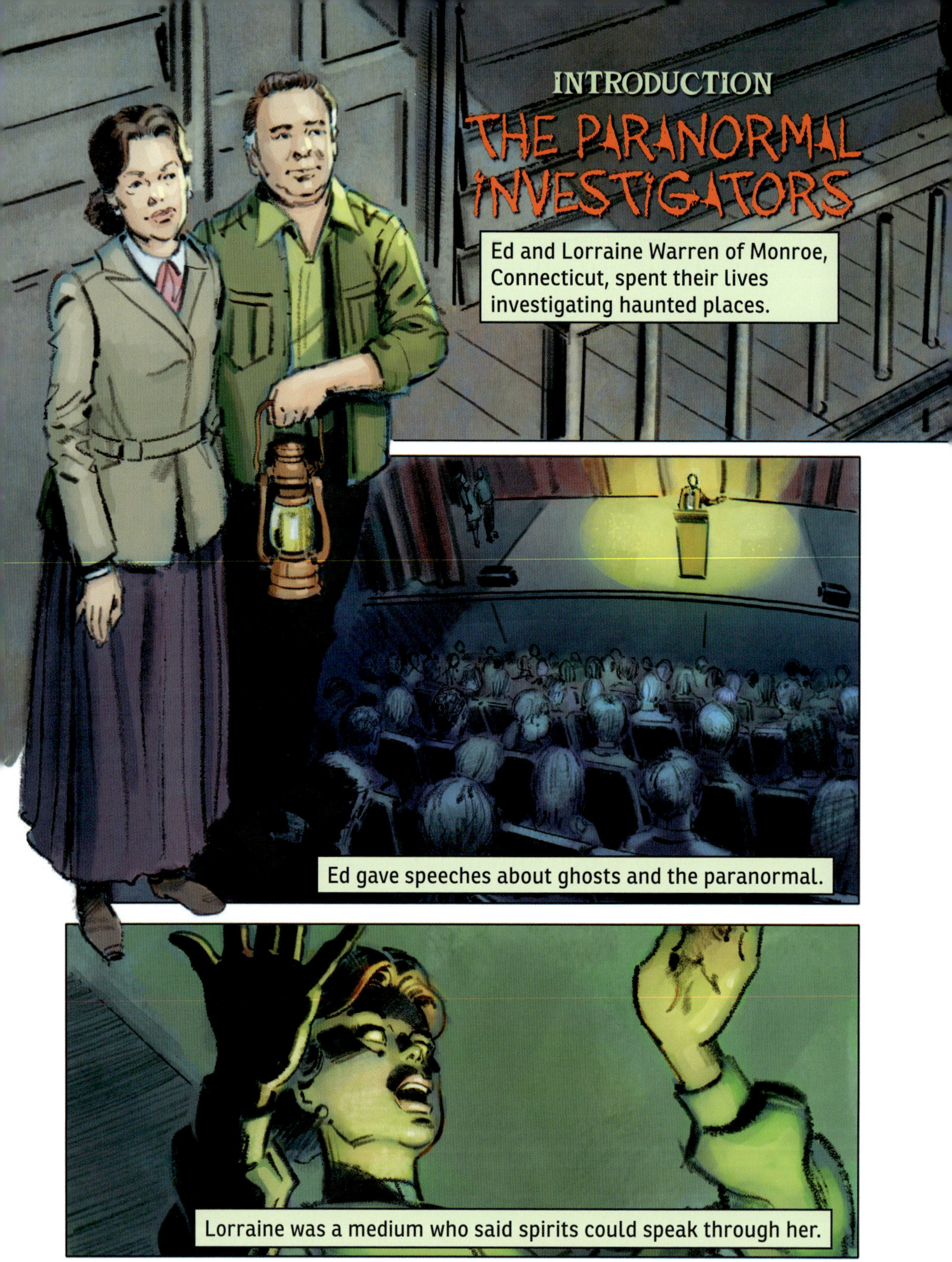
INTRODUCTION
THE PARANORMAL INVESTIGATORS
Ed and Lorraine Warren of Monroe, Connecticut, spent their lives investigating haunted places.
Ed gave speeches about ghosts and the paranormal.
Lorraine was a medium who said spirits could speak through her.

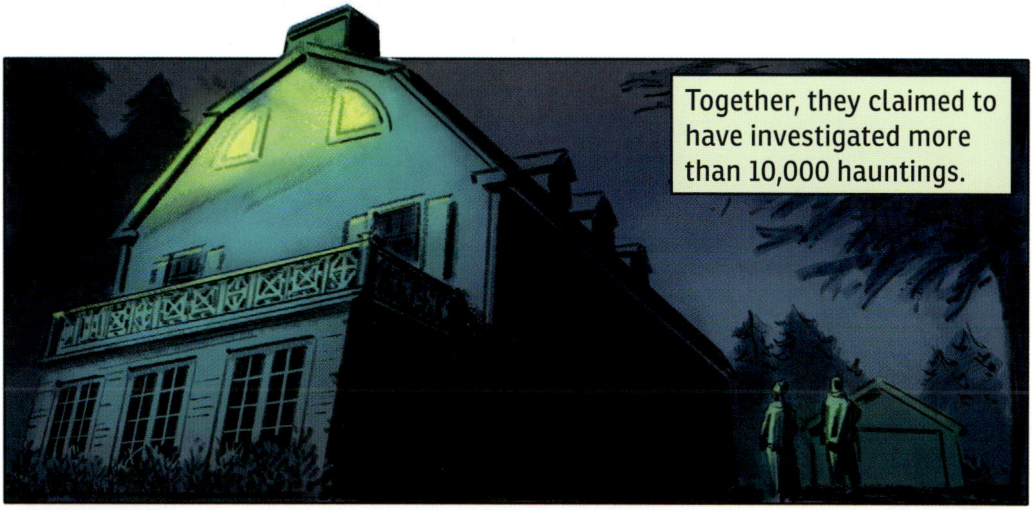
Together, they claimed to have investigated more than 10,000 hauntings.

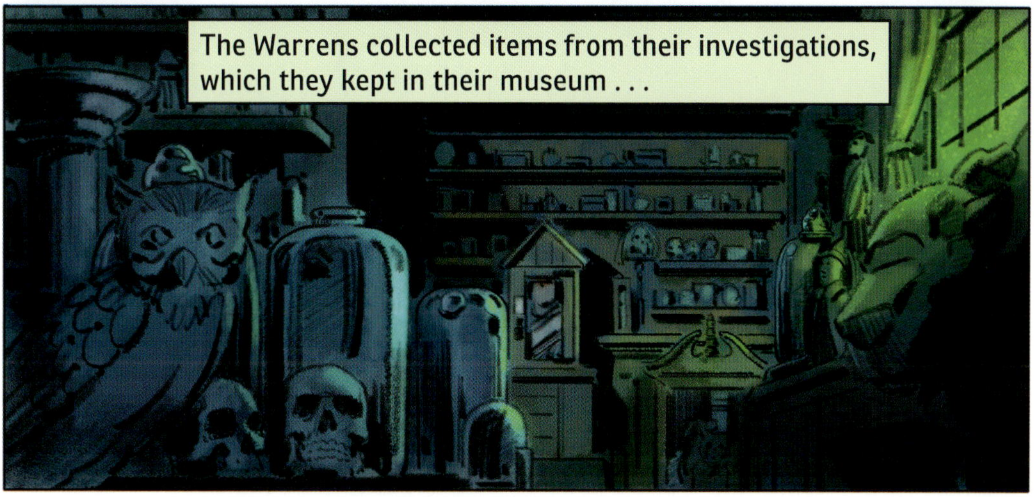
The Warrens collected items from their investigations, which they kept in their museum . . .

. . . including a doll with a terrifying history.

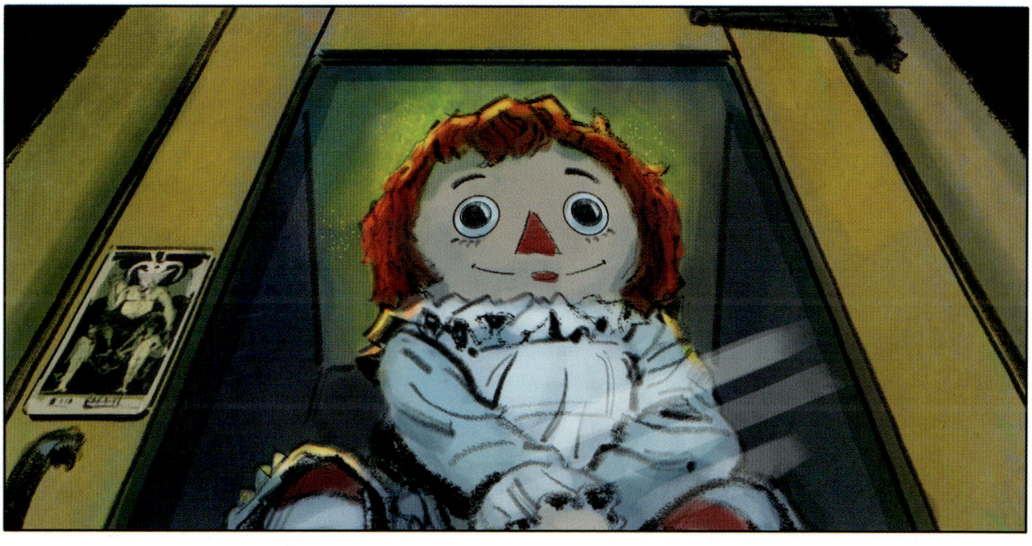

CHAPTER 1
THE NURSES

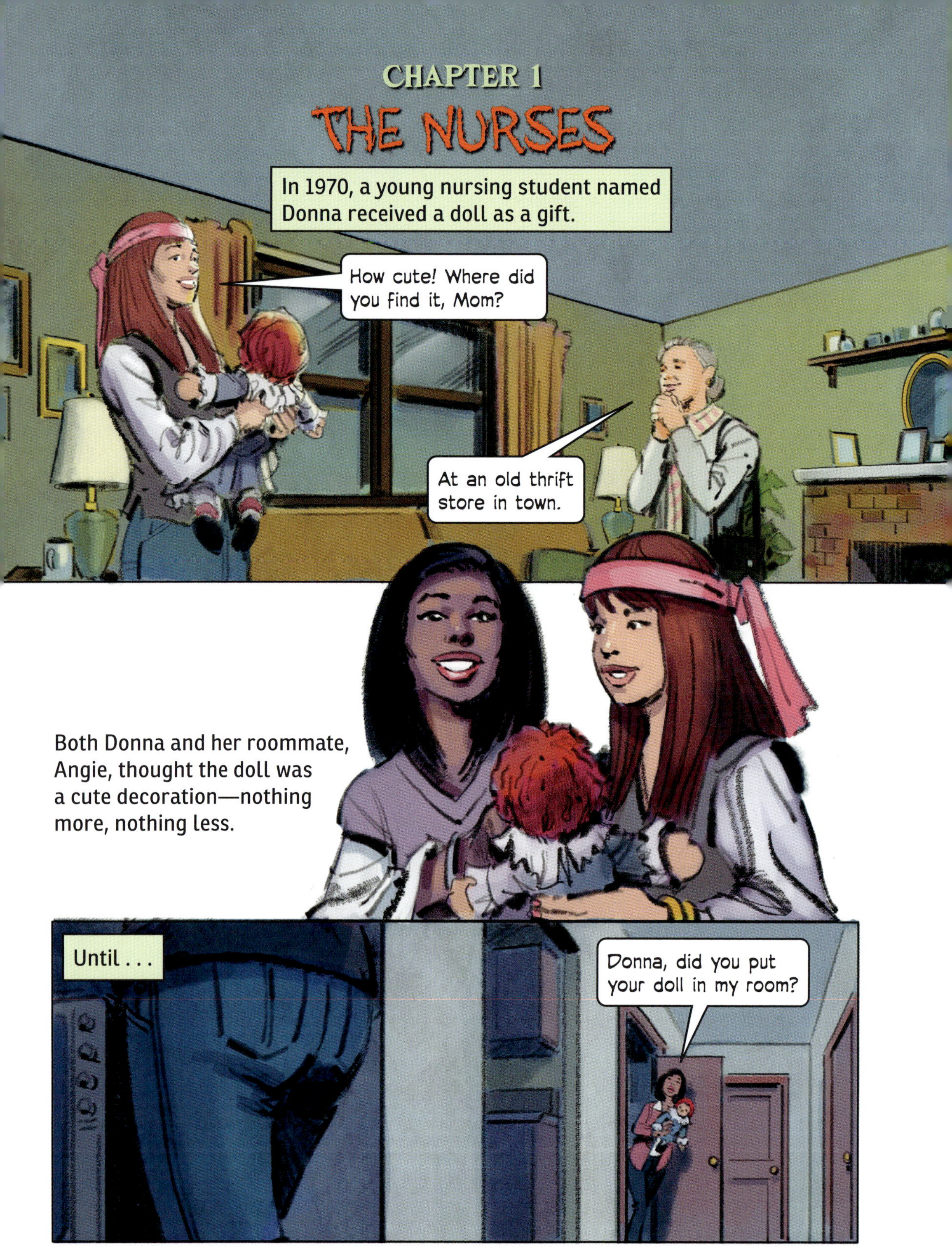
In 1970, a young nursing student named Donna received a doll as a gift.
How cute! Where did you find it, Mom?
At an old thrift store in town.
Both Donna and her roommate, Angie, thought the doll was a cute decoration—nothing more, nothing less.
Until . . .
Donna, did you put your doll in my room?

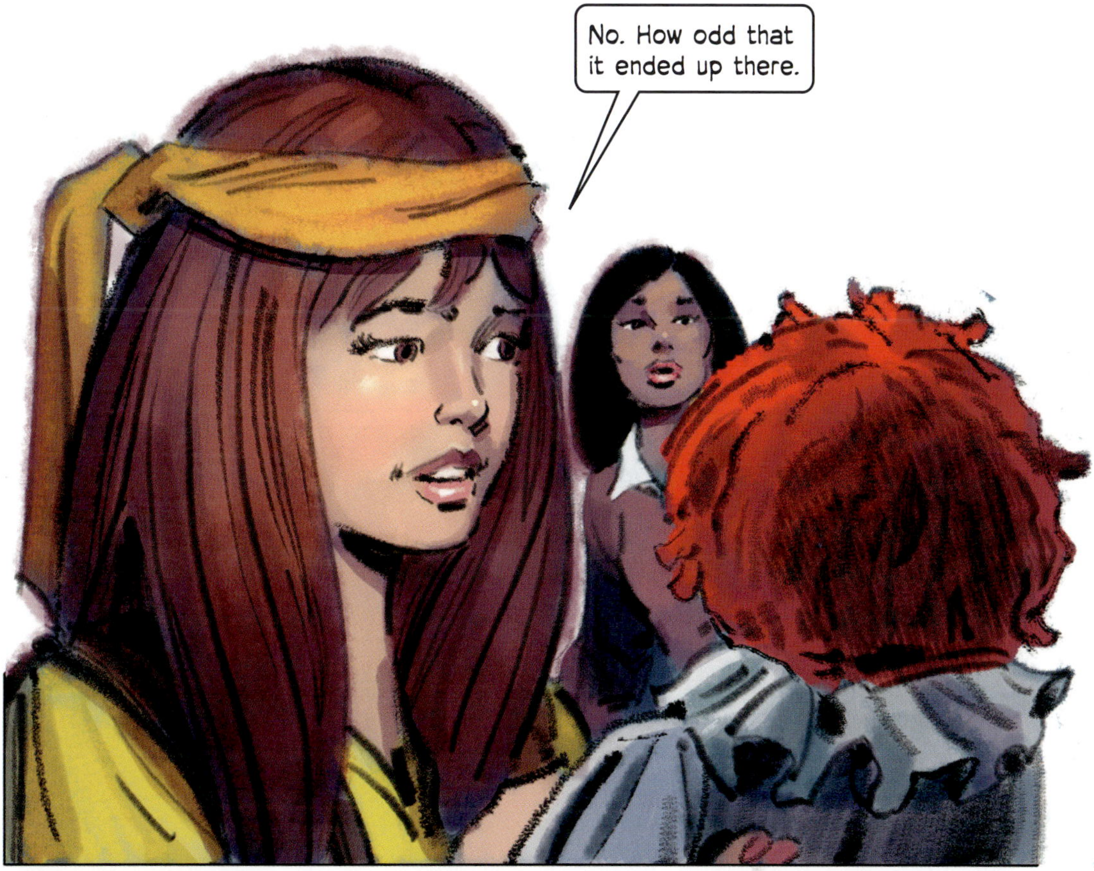
No. How odd that it ended up there.

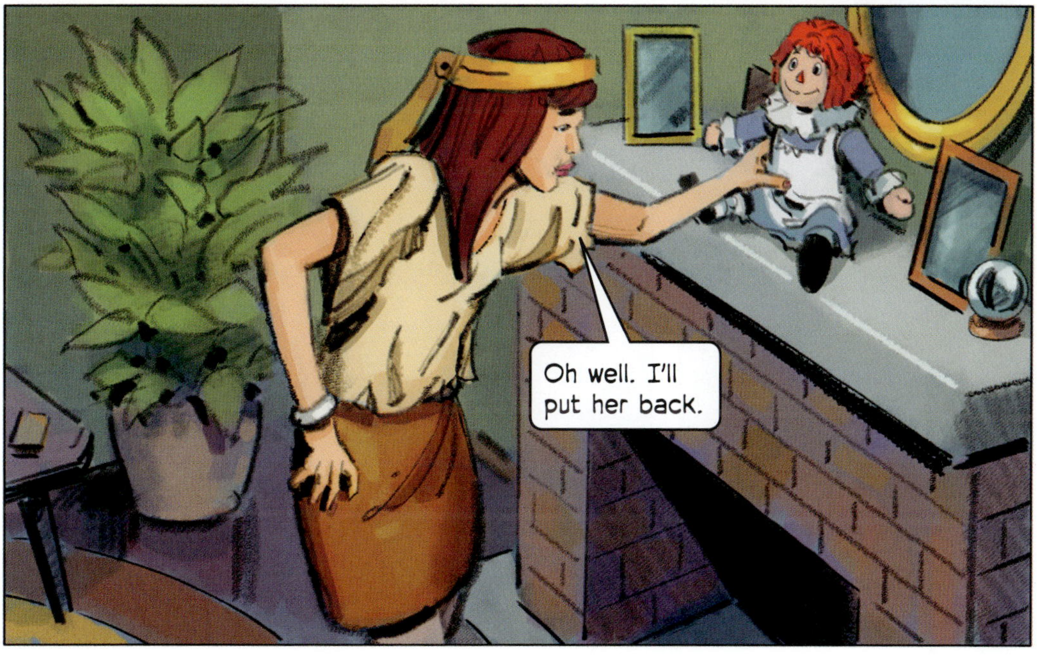
Oh well. I'll put her back.

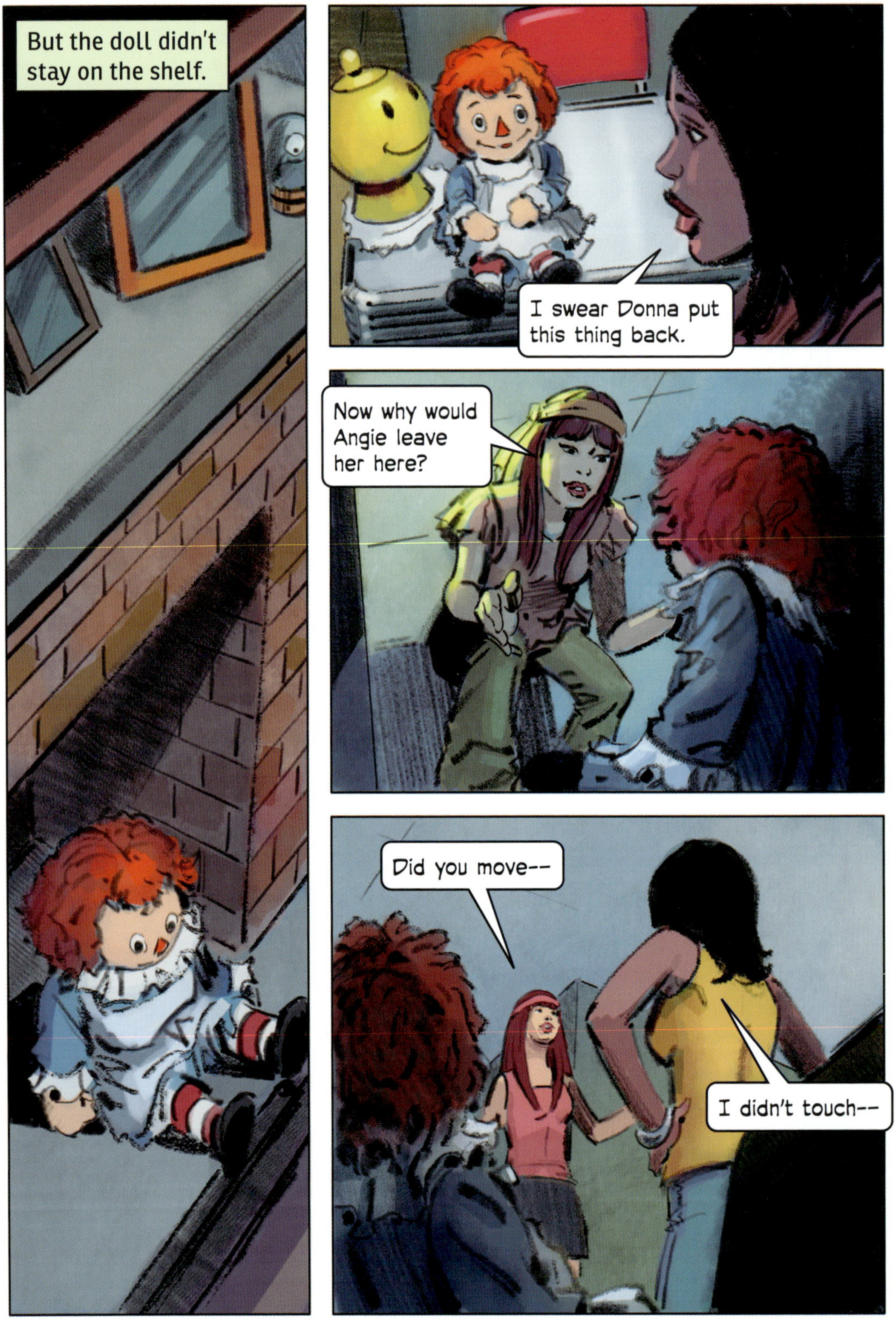
But the doll didn't stay on the shelf.
I swear Donna put this thing back.
Now why would Angie leave her here?
Did you move--
I didn't touch--

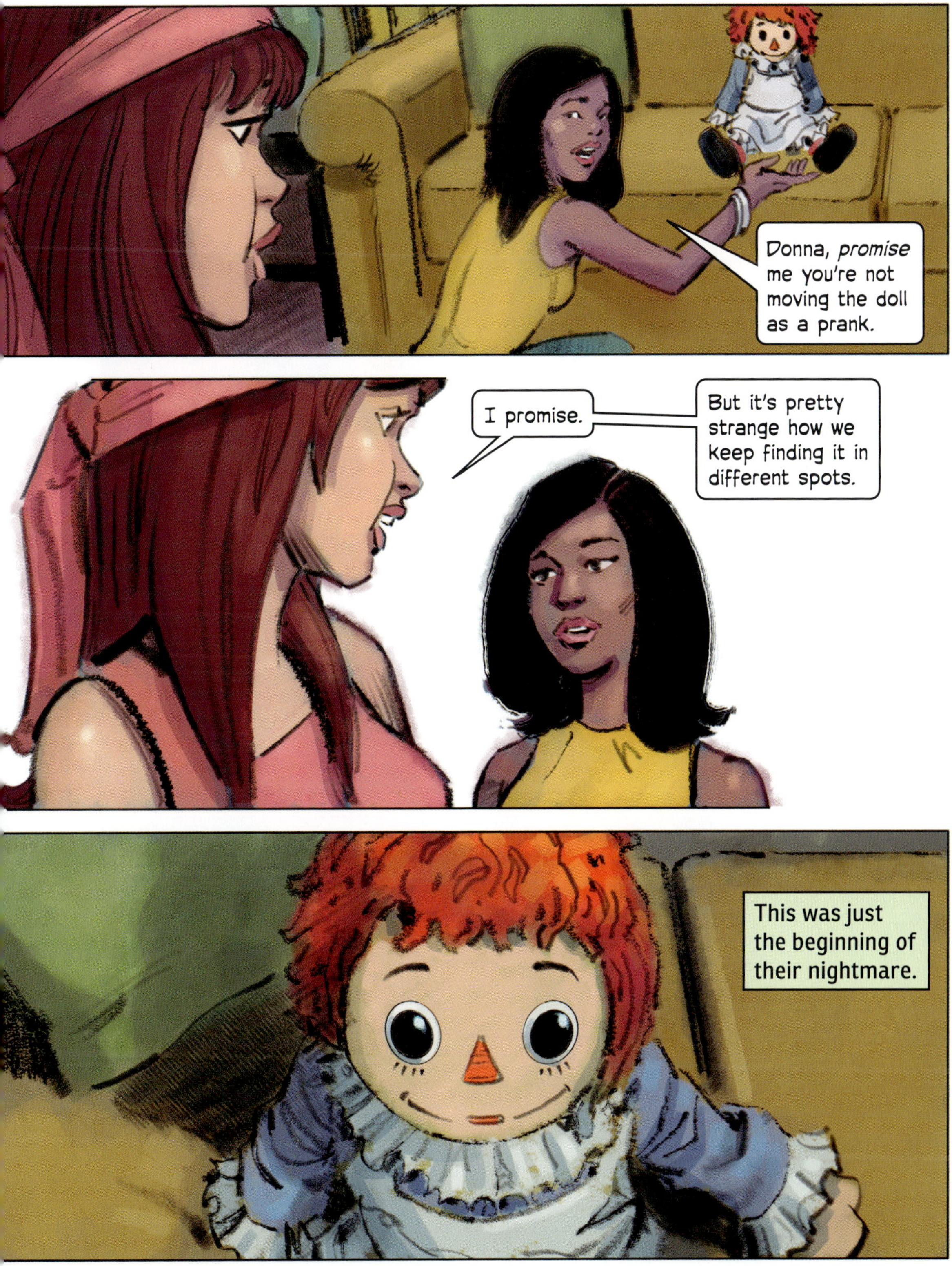

Donna, *promise* me you're not moving the doll as a prank.
I promise.
But it's pretty strange how we keep finding it in different spots.
This was just the beginning of their nightmare.

Angie's boyfriend, Lou, had a bad feeling about the doll from the start.

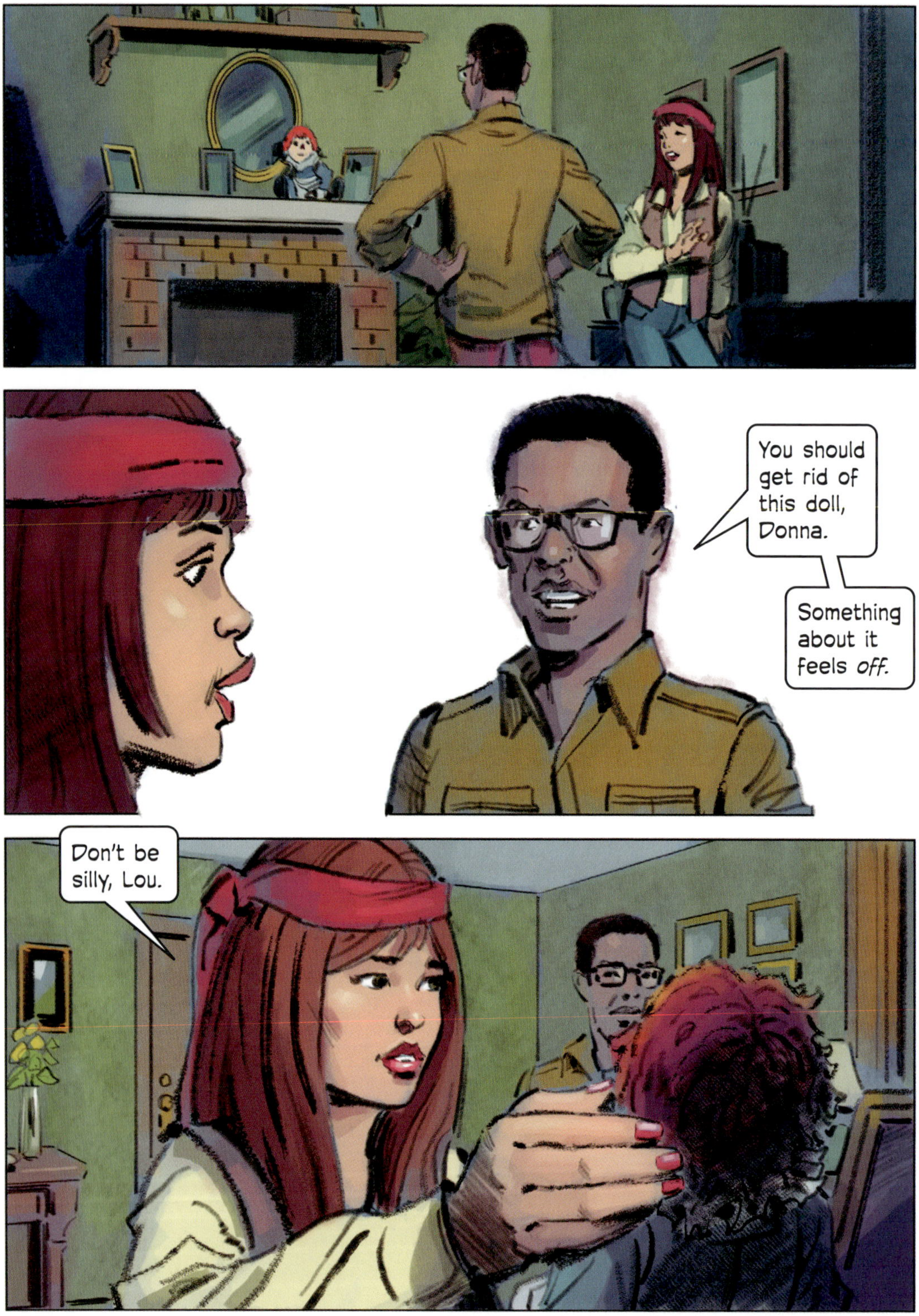

You should get rid of this doll, Donna.
Something about it feels *off*.
Don't be silly, Lou.

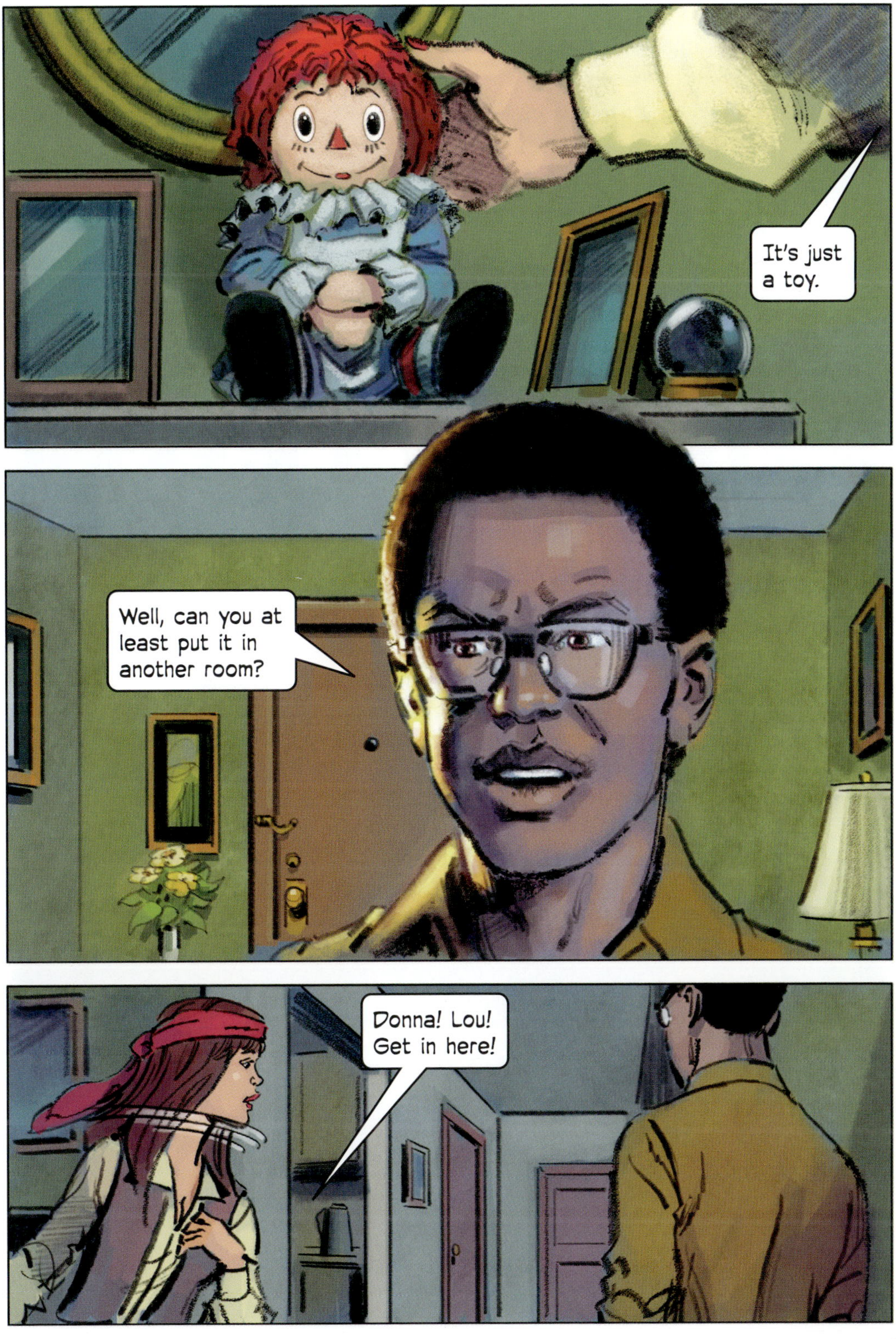
It's just a toy.
Well, can you at least put it in another room?
Donna! Lou! Get in here!

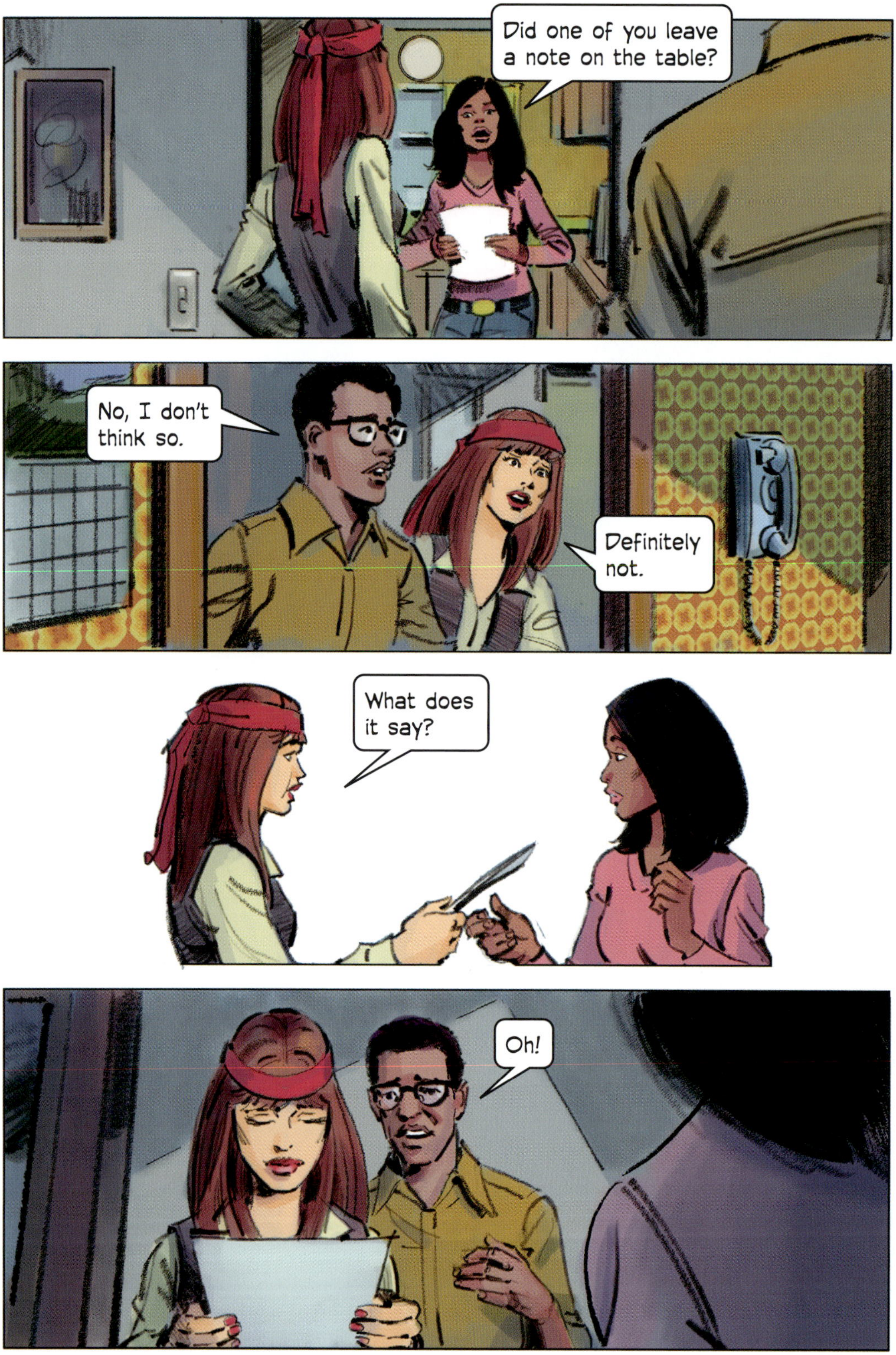
Did one of you leave a note on the table?
No, I don't think so.
Definitely not.
What does it say?
Oh!

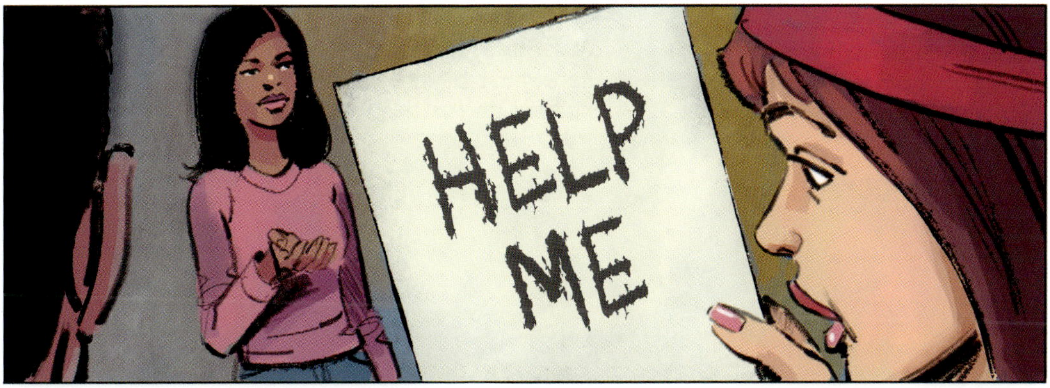
HELP ME

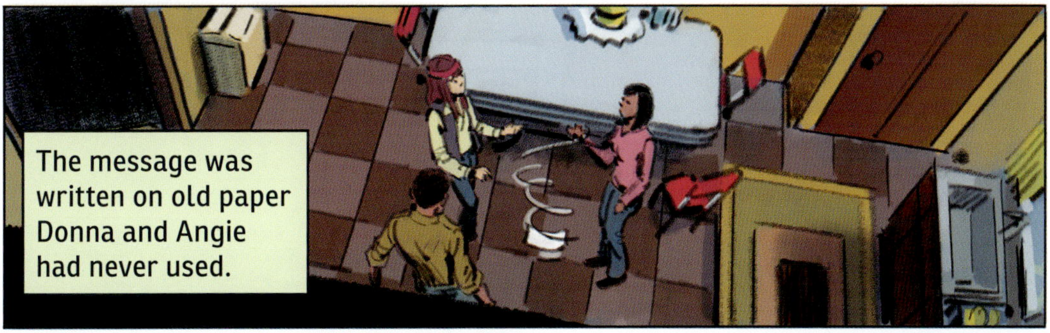
The message was written on old paper Donna and Angie had never used.

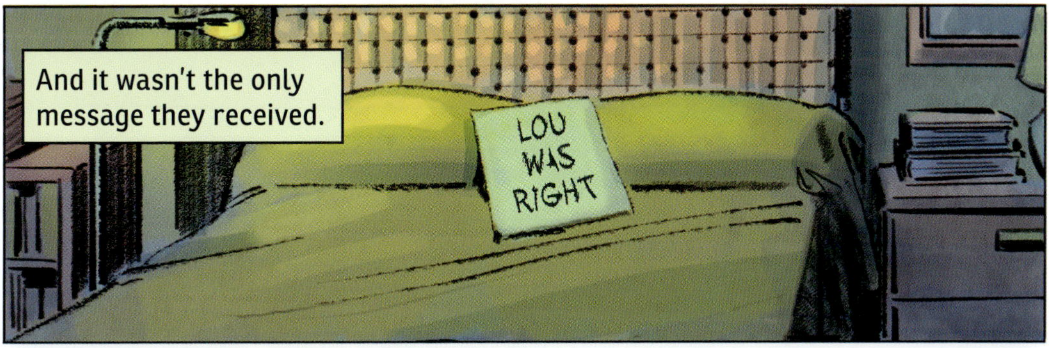
And it wasn't the only message they received.
LOU WAS RIGHT

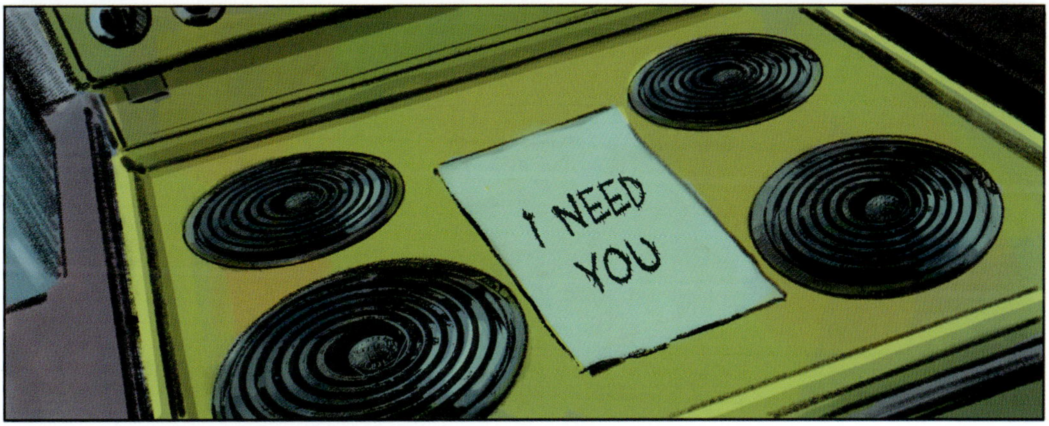
I NEED YOU

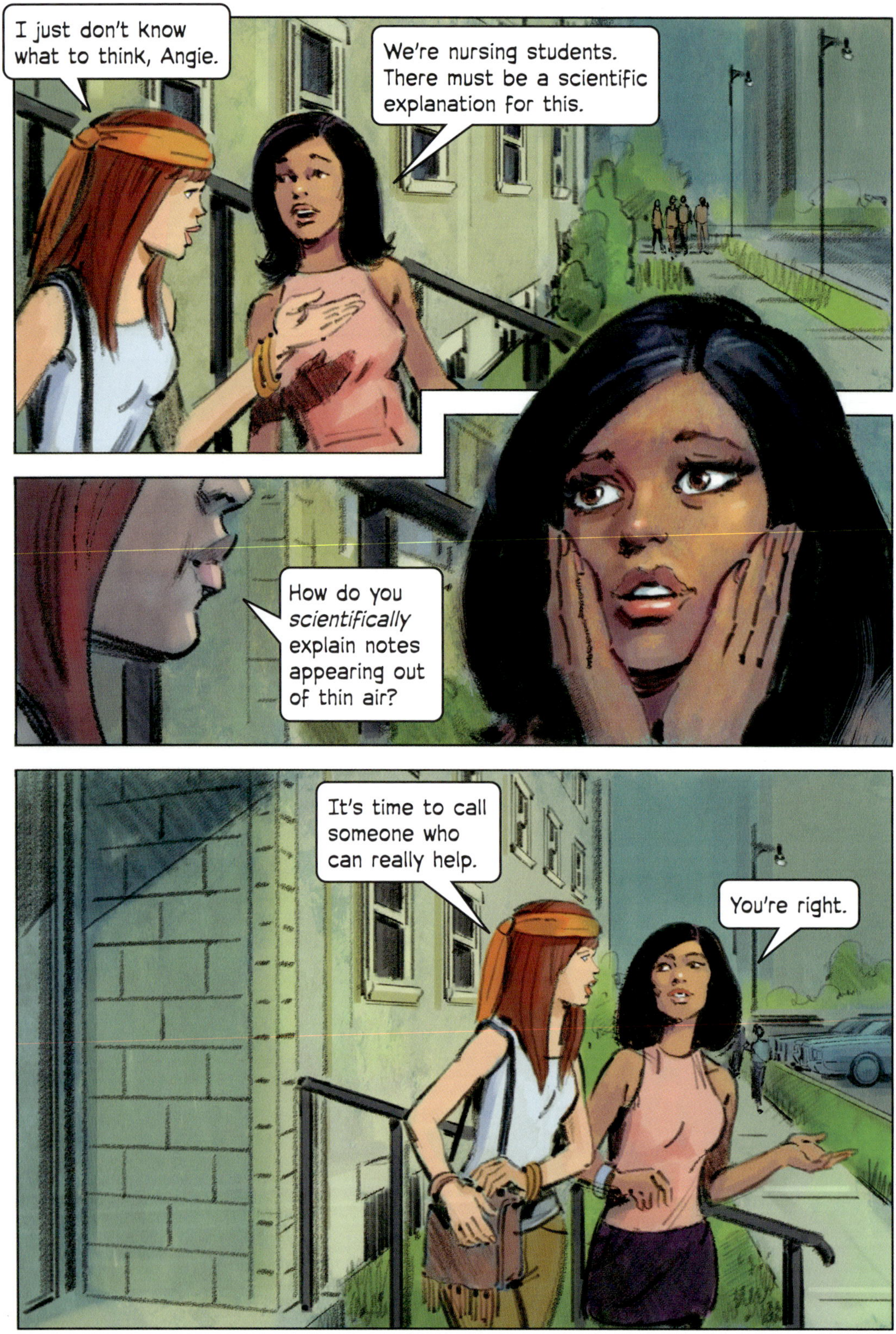
I just don't know what to think, Angie.
We're nursing students. There must be a scientific explanation for this.
How do you *scientifically* explain notes appearing out of thin air?
It's time to call someone who can really help.
You're right.

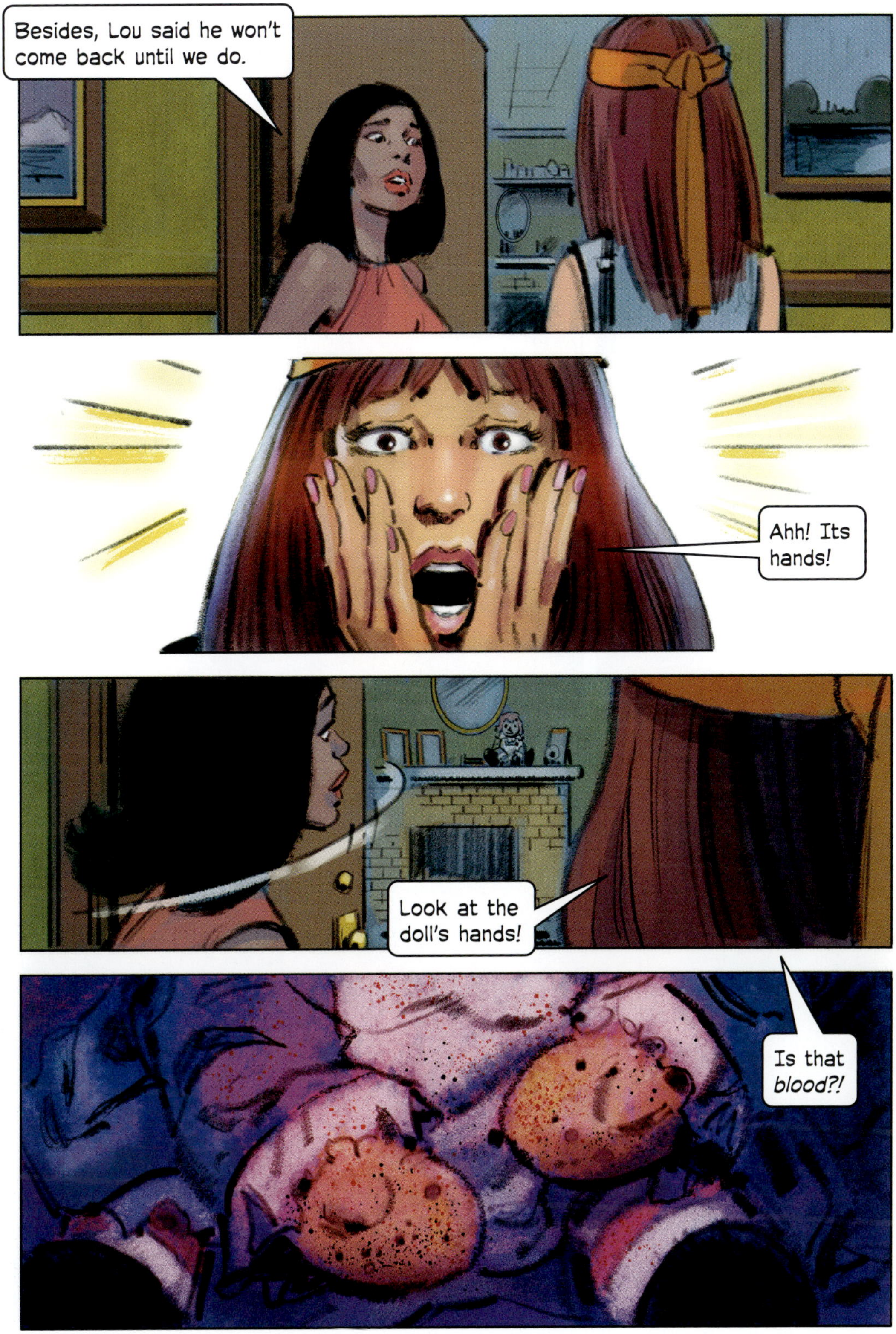
Besides, Lou said he won't come back until we do.
Ahh! Its hands!
Look at the doll's hands!
Is that *blood?!*

CHAPTER 2

THE GIRL IN THE FIELD

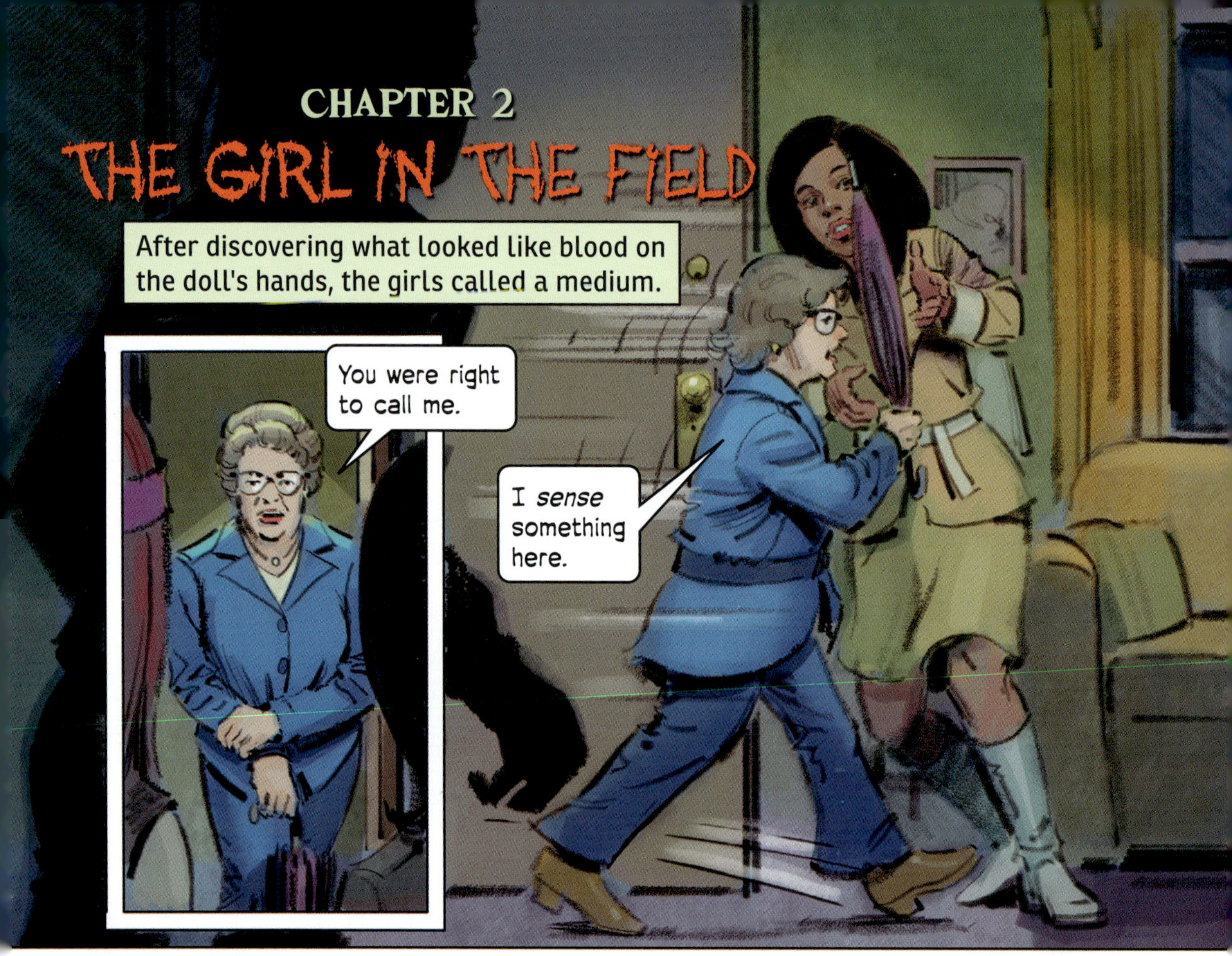
After discovering what looked like blood on the doll's hands, the girls called a medium.
You were right to call me.
I *sense* something here.

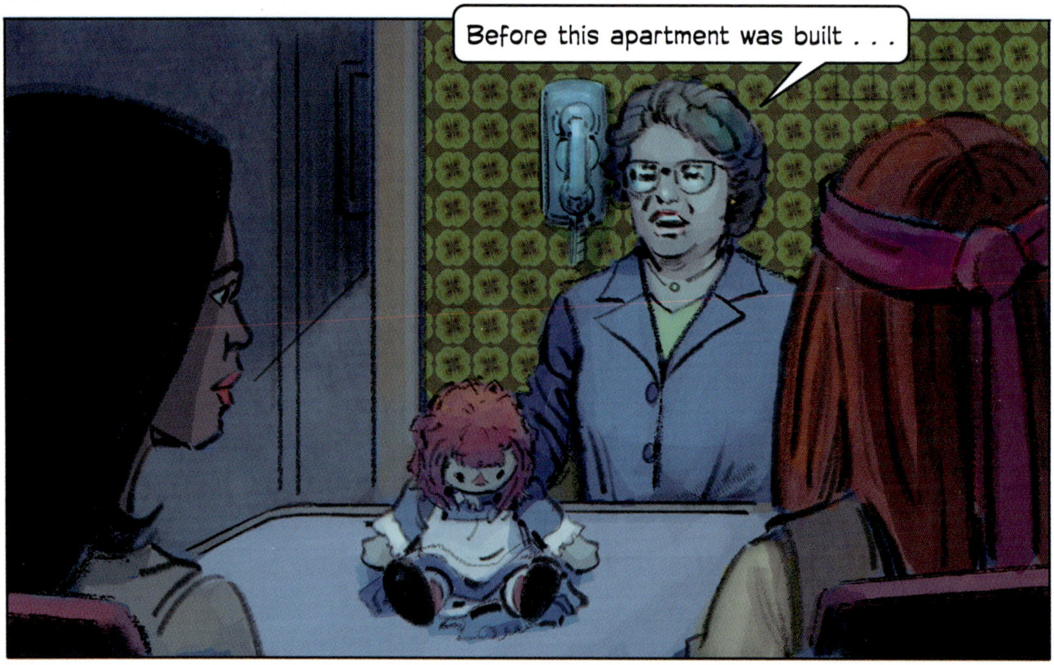
Before this apartment was built . . .

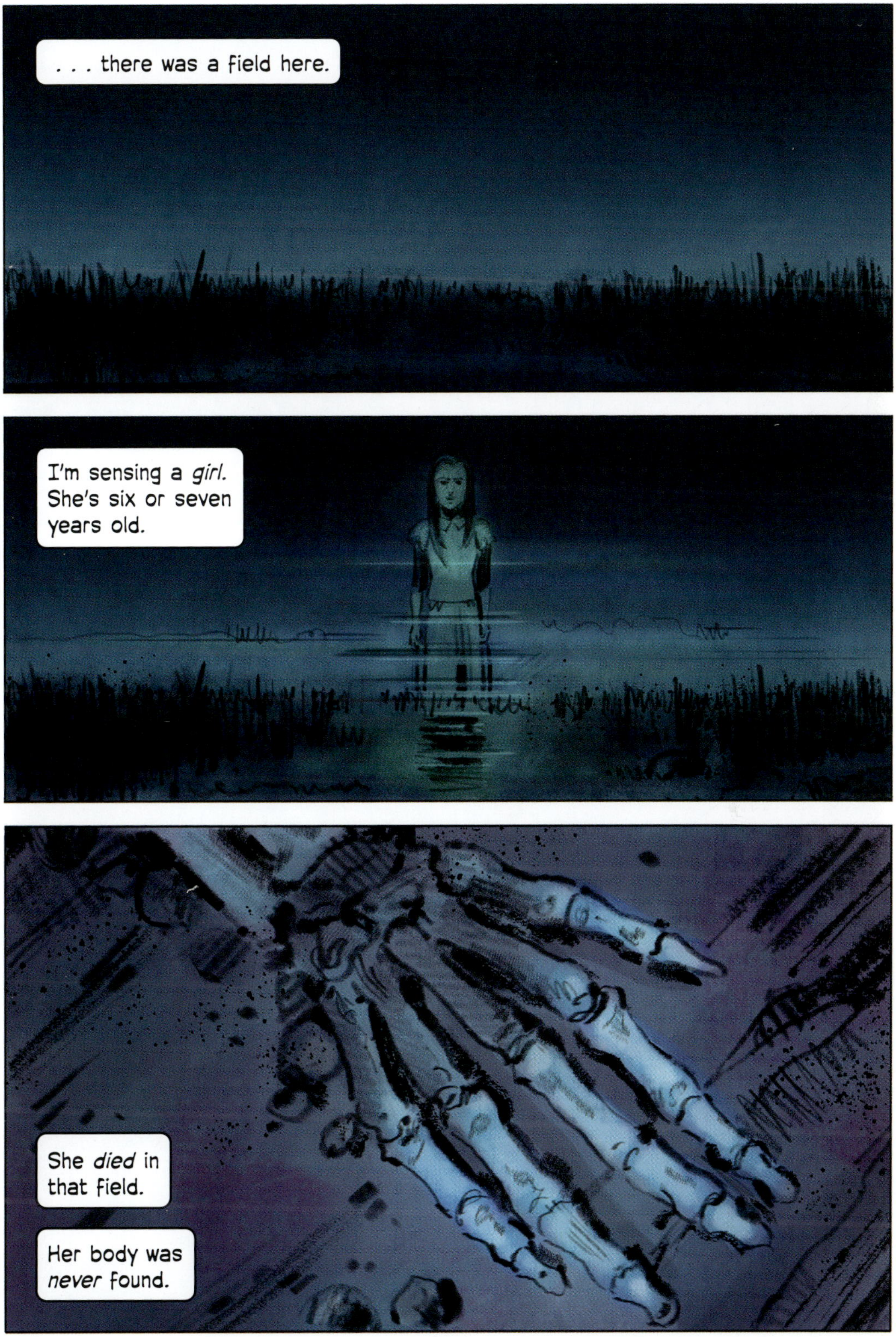
. . . there was a field here.
I'm sensing a *girl.* She's six or seven years old.
She *died* in that field.
Her body was *never* found.

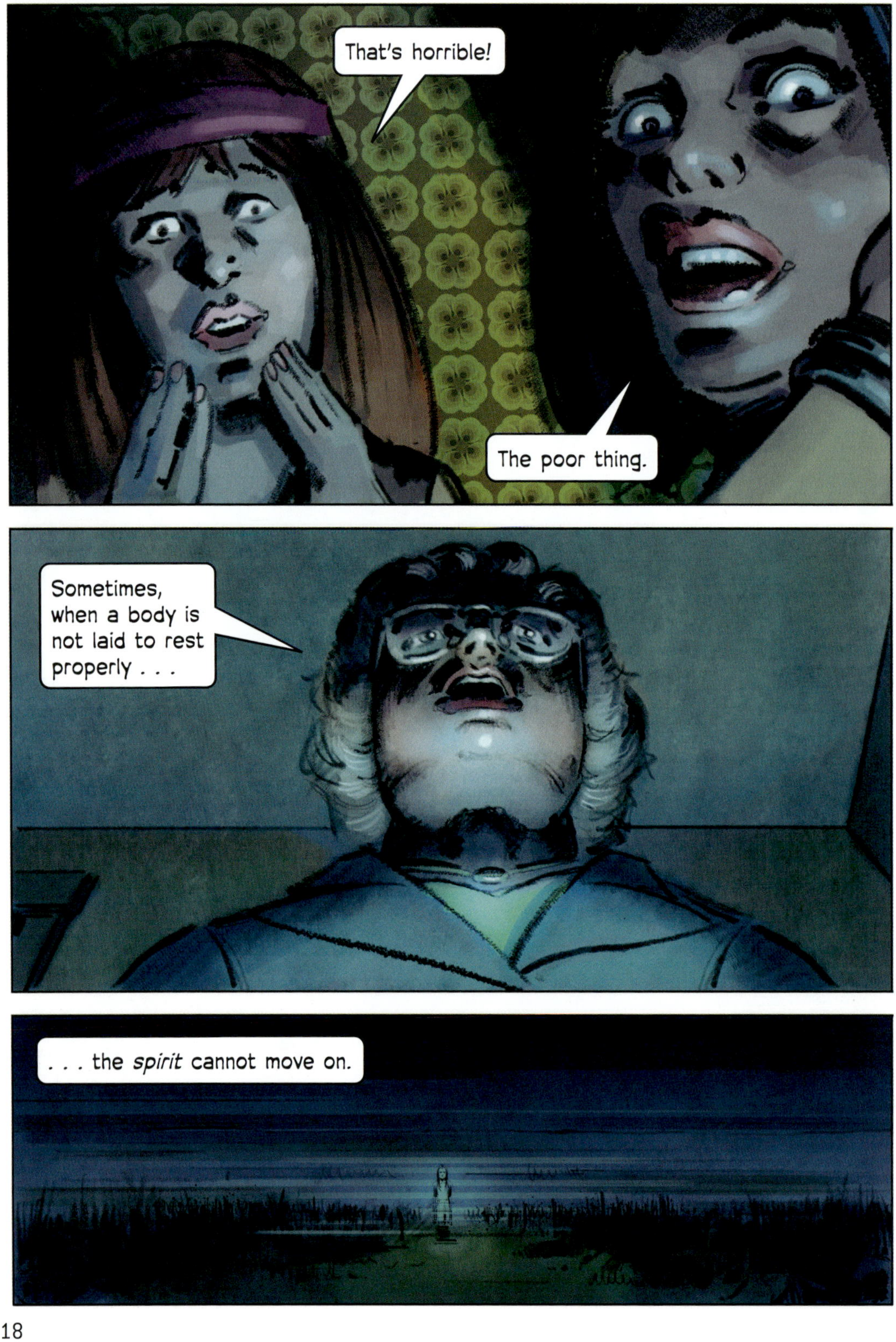
That's horrible!
The poor thing.
Sometimes, when a body is not laid to rest properly . . .
. . . the *spirit* cannot move on.

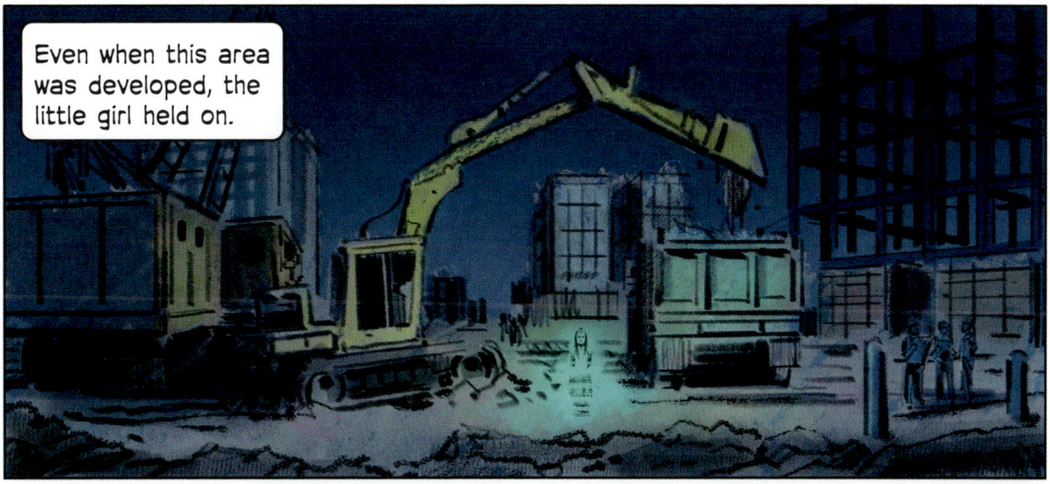
Even when this area was developed, the little girl held on.

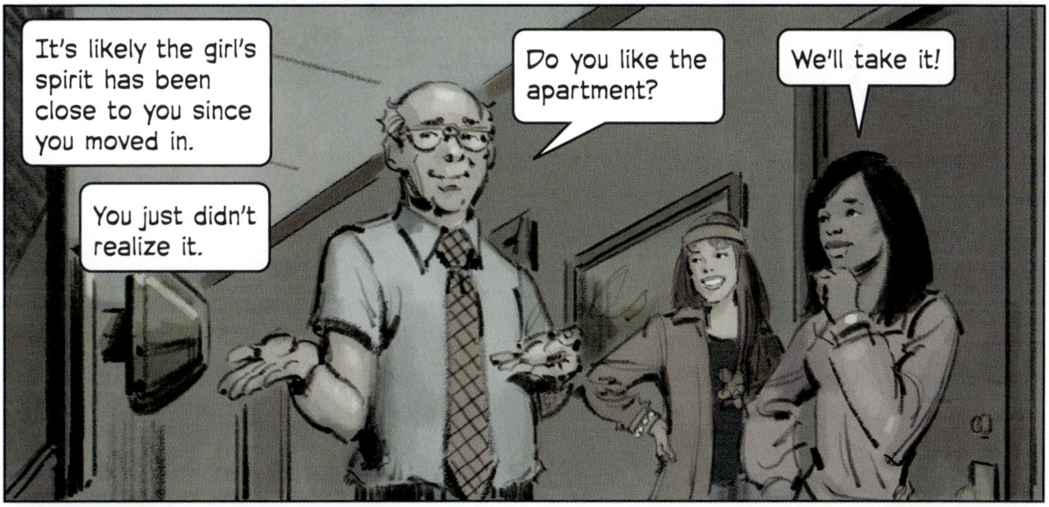
It's likely the girl's spirit has been close to you since you moved in.
You just didn't realize it.
Do you like the apartment?
We'll take it!

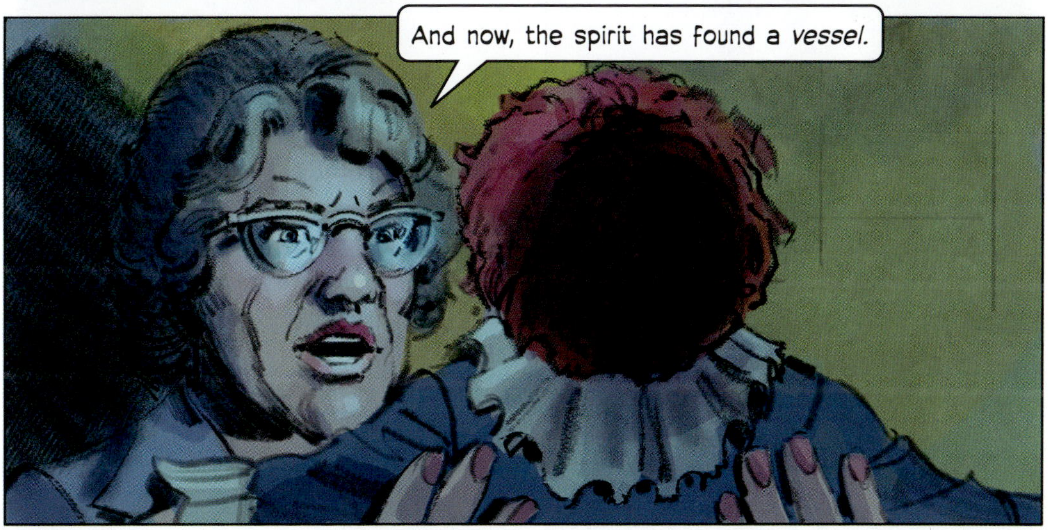
And now, the spirit has found a *vessel.*

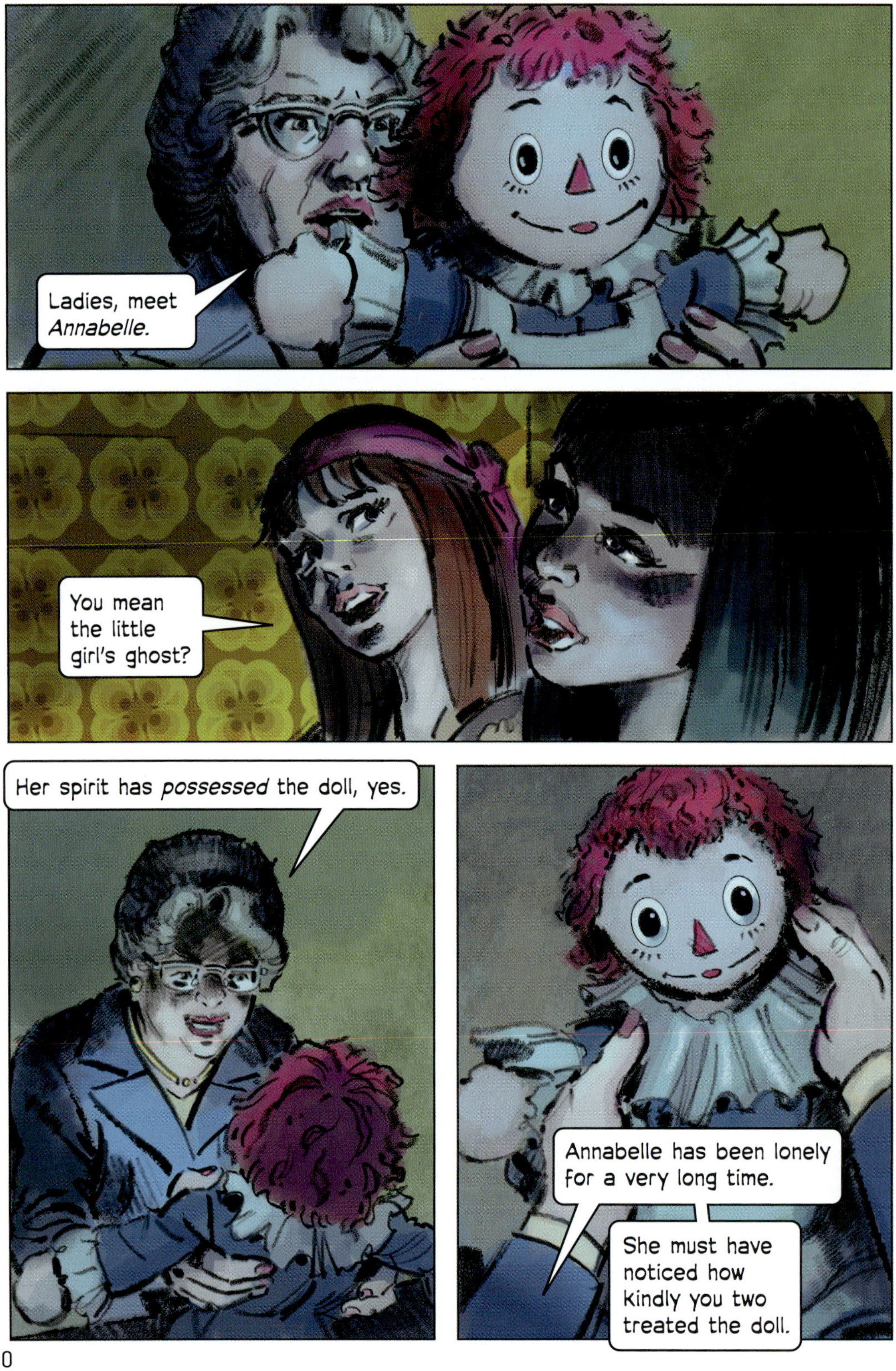
Ladies, meet *Annabelle.*
You mean the little girl's ghost?
Her spirit has *possessed* the doll, yes.
Annabelle has been lonely for a very long time.
She must have noticed how kindly you two treated the doll.

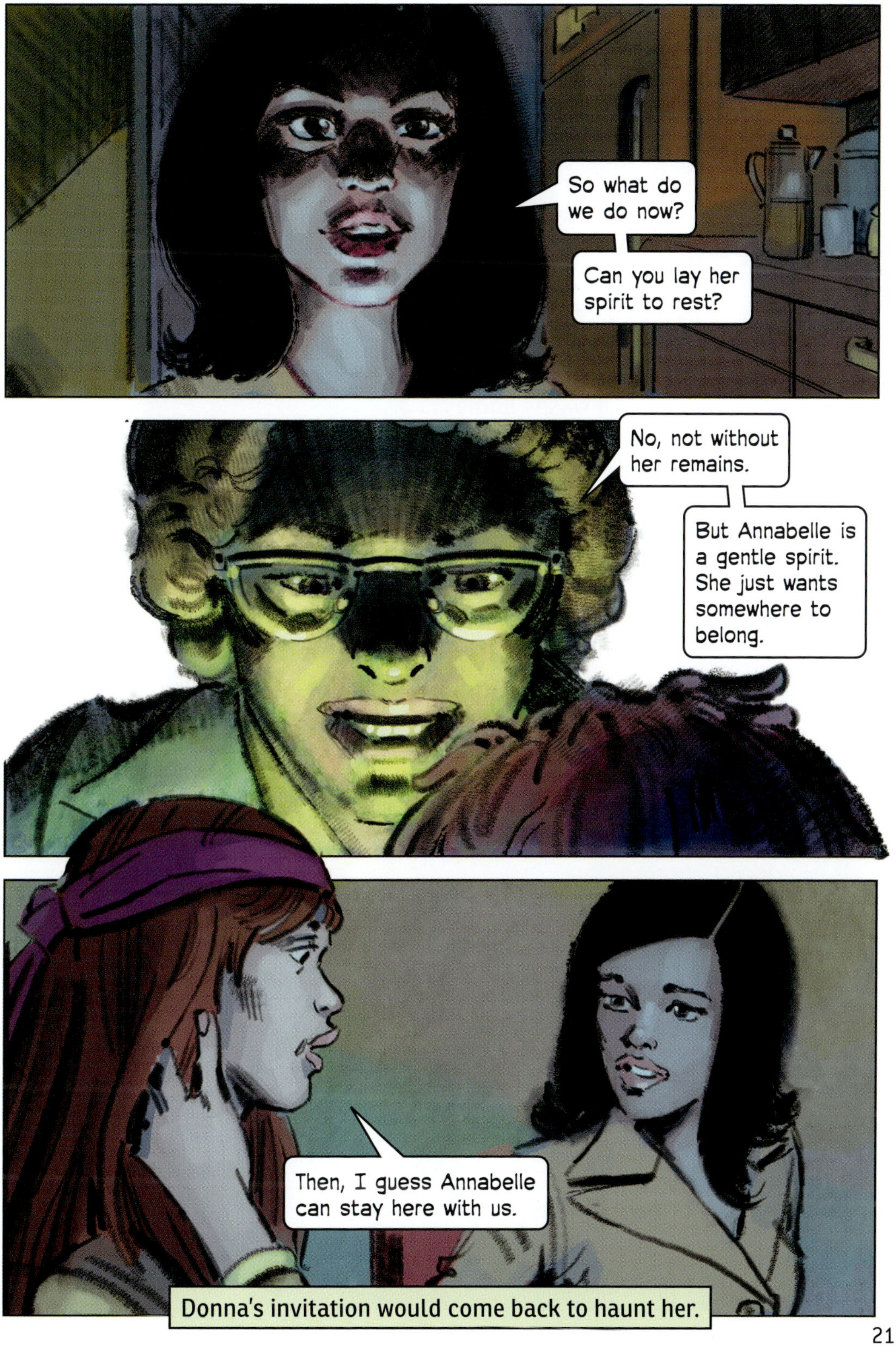
So what do we do now?
Can you lay her spirit to rest?
No, not without her remains.
But Annabelle is a gentle spirit. She just wants somewhere to belong.
Then, I guess Annabelle can stay here with us.
Donna's invitation would come back to haunt her.

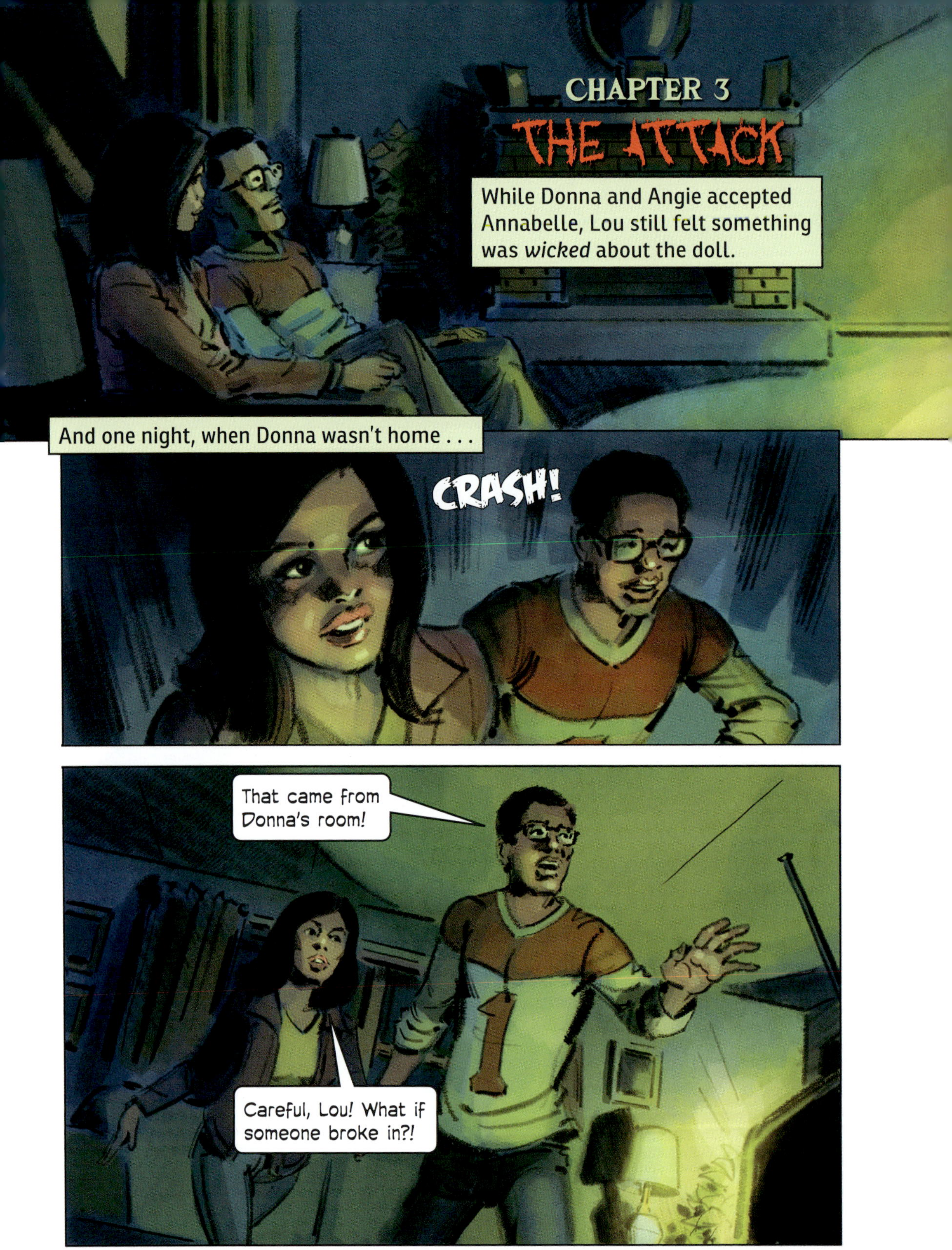
CHAPTER 3
THE ATTACK
While Donna and Angie accepted Annabelle, Lou still felt something was *wicked* about the doll.
And one night, when Donna wasn't home . . .
CRASH!
That came from Donna's room!
Careful, Lou! What if someone broke in?!

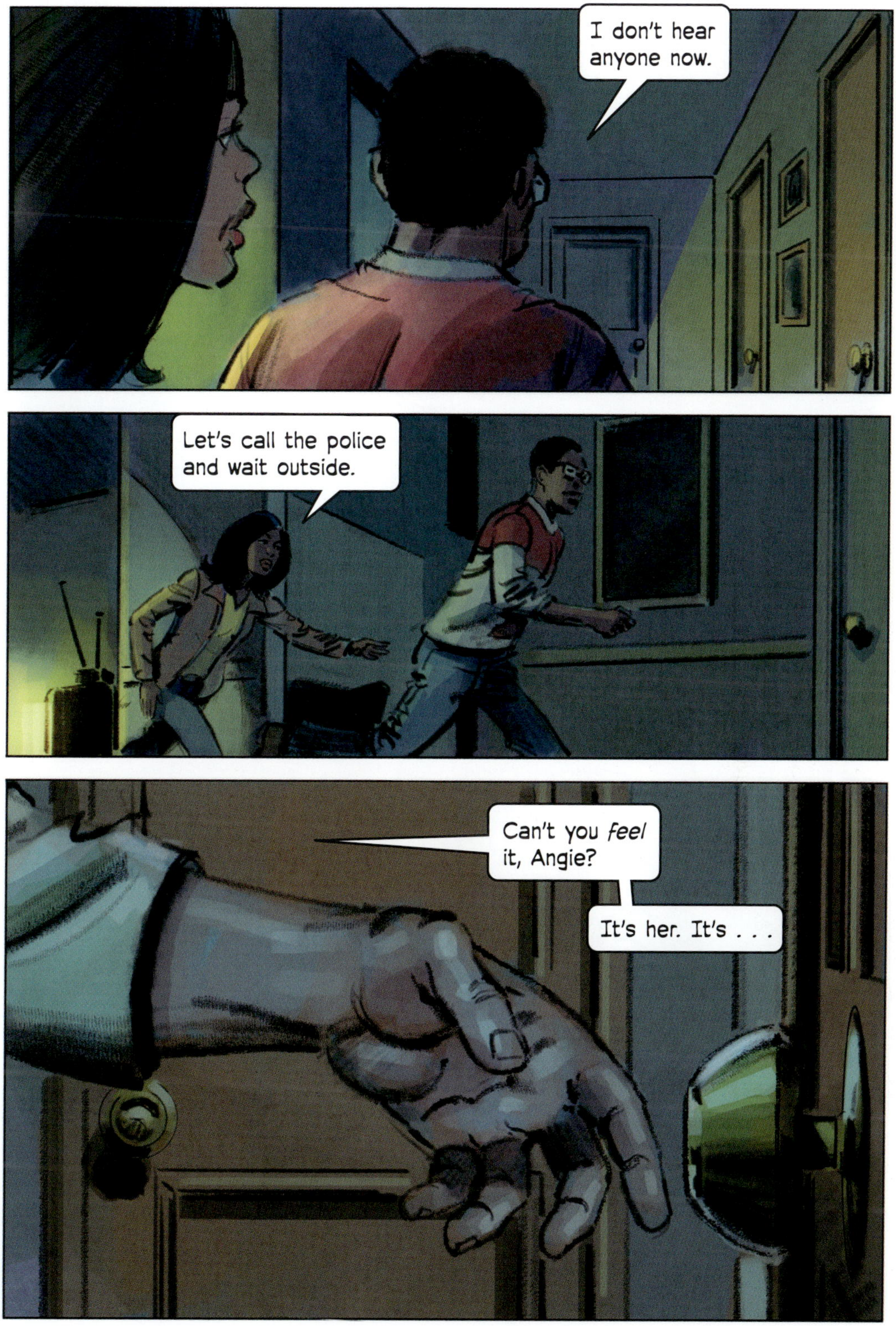
I don't hear anyone now.
Let's call the police and wait outside.
Can't you *feel* it, Angie?
It's her. It's . . .

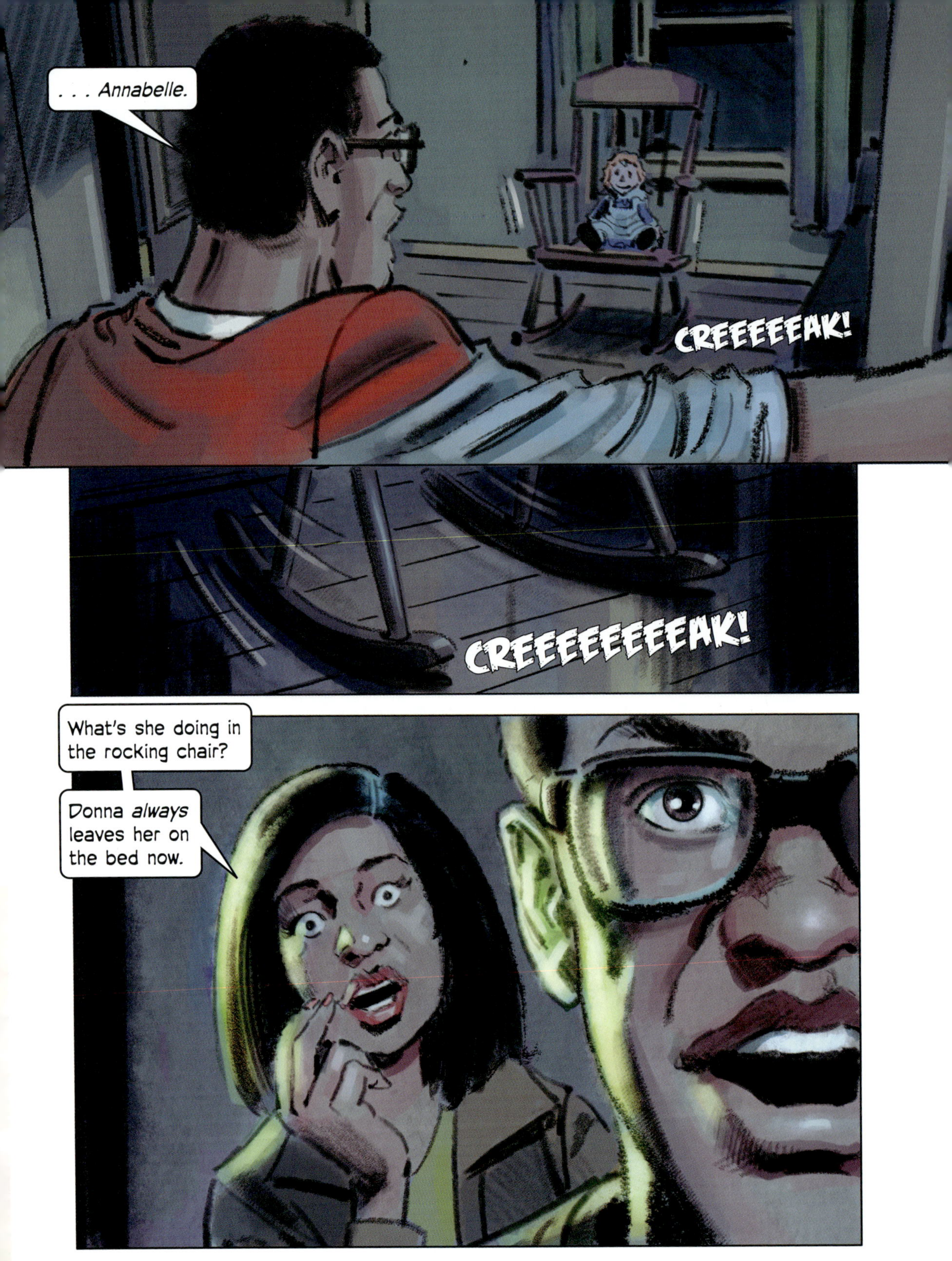
. . . Annabelle.
CREEEEEAK!
CREEEEEEEEAK!
What's she doing in the rocking chair?
Donna *always* leaves her on the bed now.

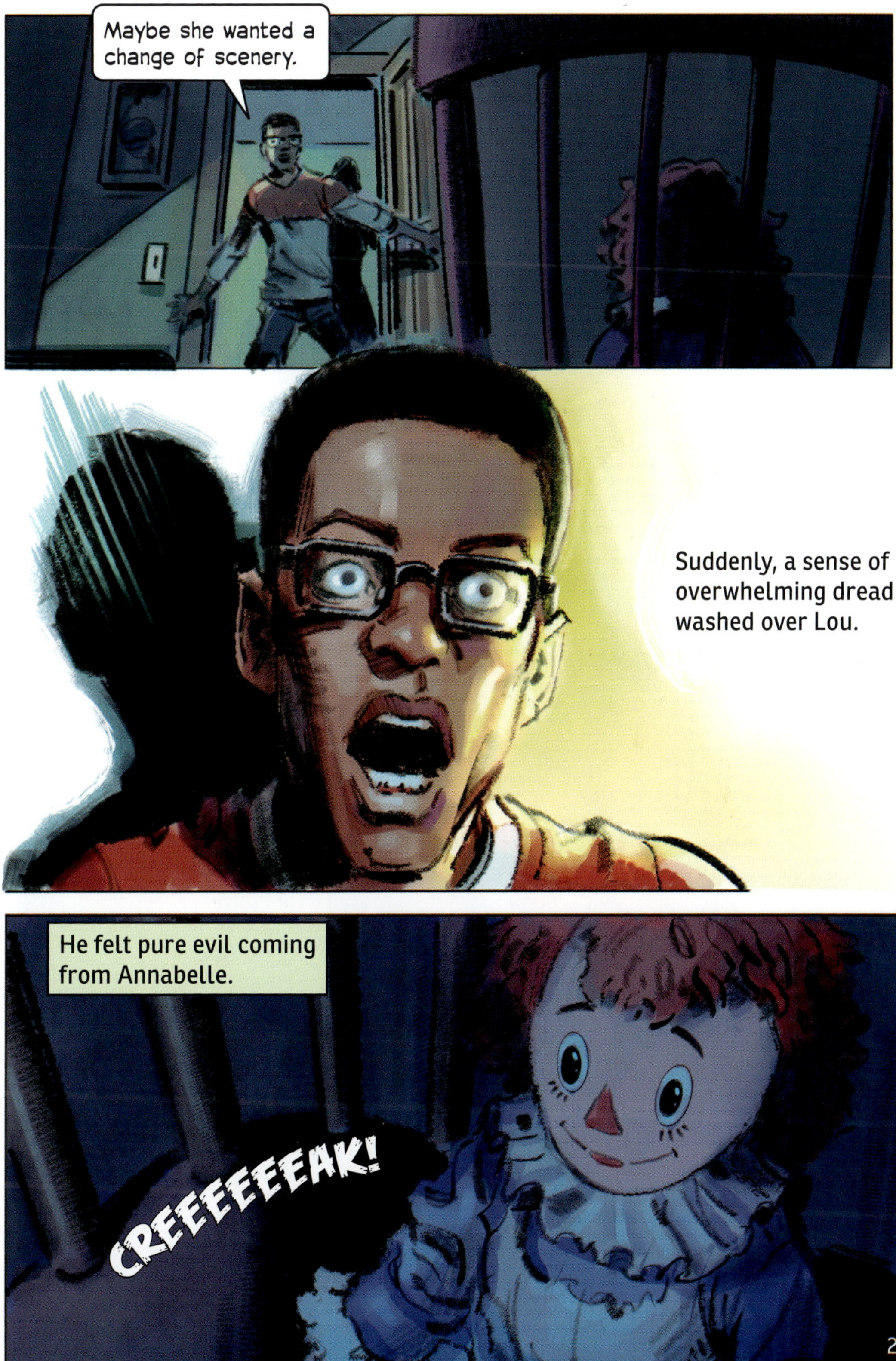
Maybe she wanted a change of scenery.
Suddenly, a sense of overwhelming dread washed over Lou.
He felt pure evil coming from Annabelle.
CREEEEEEEAK!

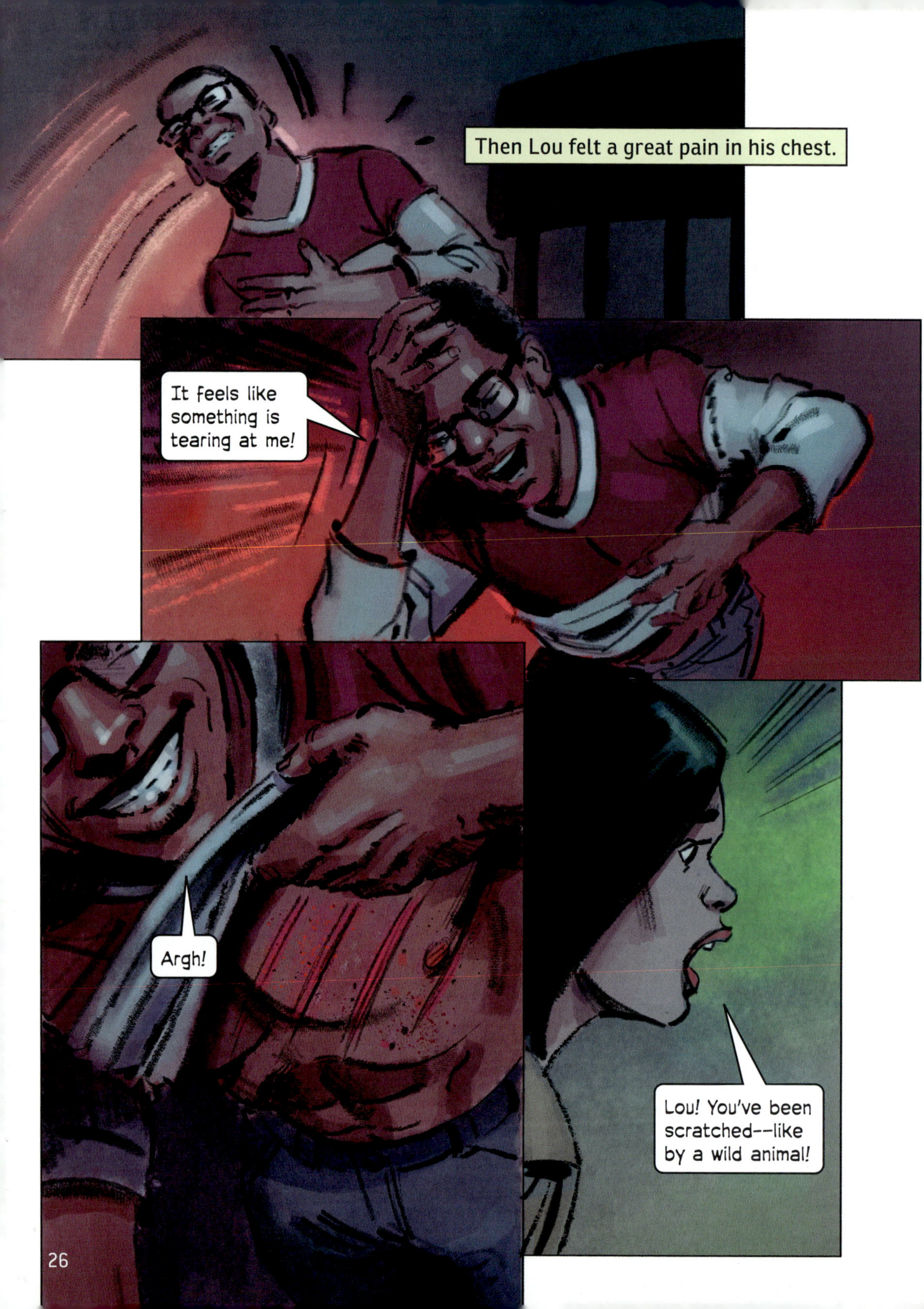
Then Lou felt a great pain in his chest.
It feels like something is tearing at me!
Argh!
Lou! You've been scratched--like by a wild animal!

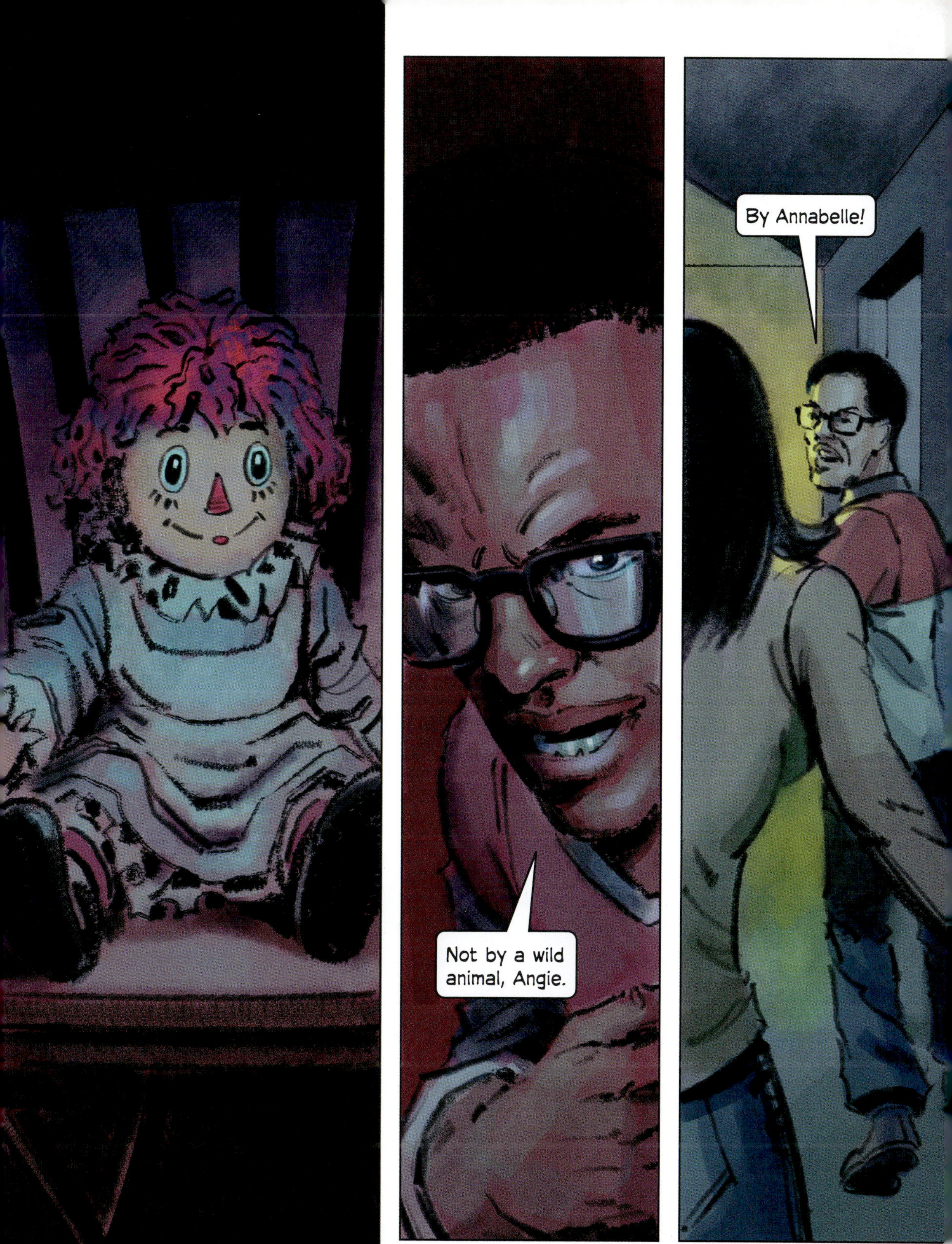
Not by a wild animal, Angie.
By Annabelle!

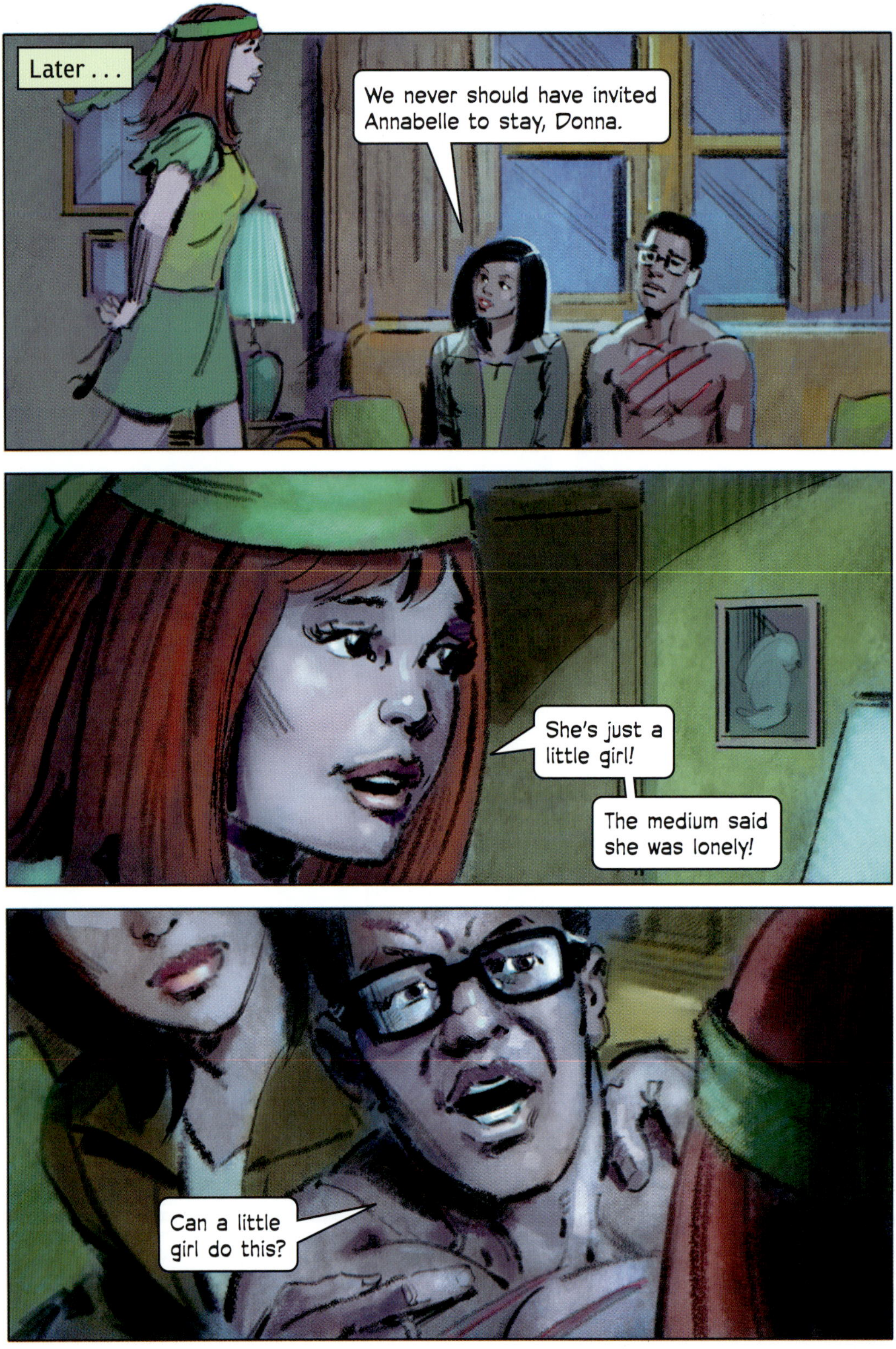
Later . . .
We never should have invited Annabelle to stay, Donna.
She's just a little girl!
The medium said she was lonely!
Can a little girl do this?

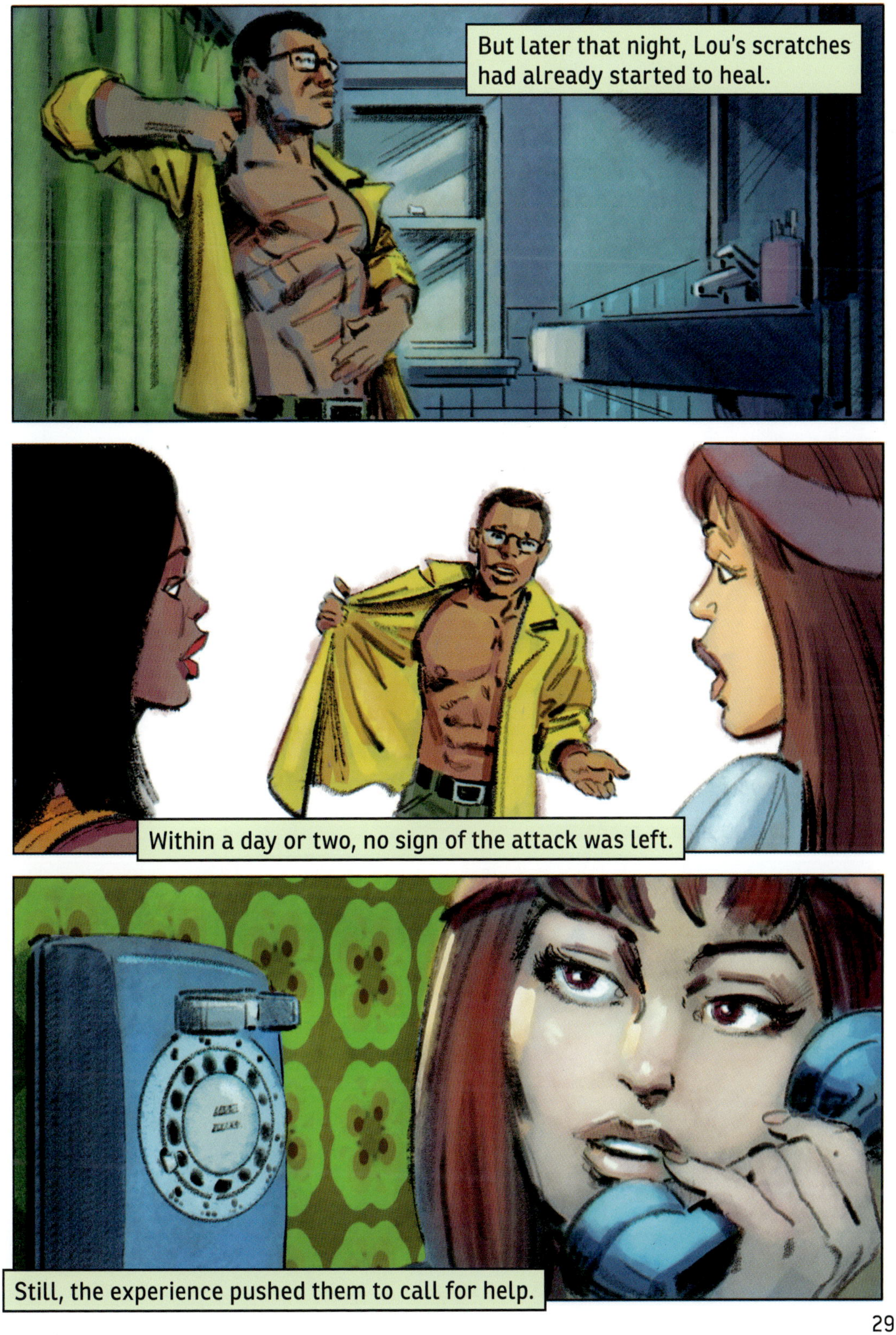
But later that night, Lou's scratches had already started to heal.
Within a day or two, no sign of the attack was left.
Still, the experience pushed them to call for help.

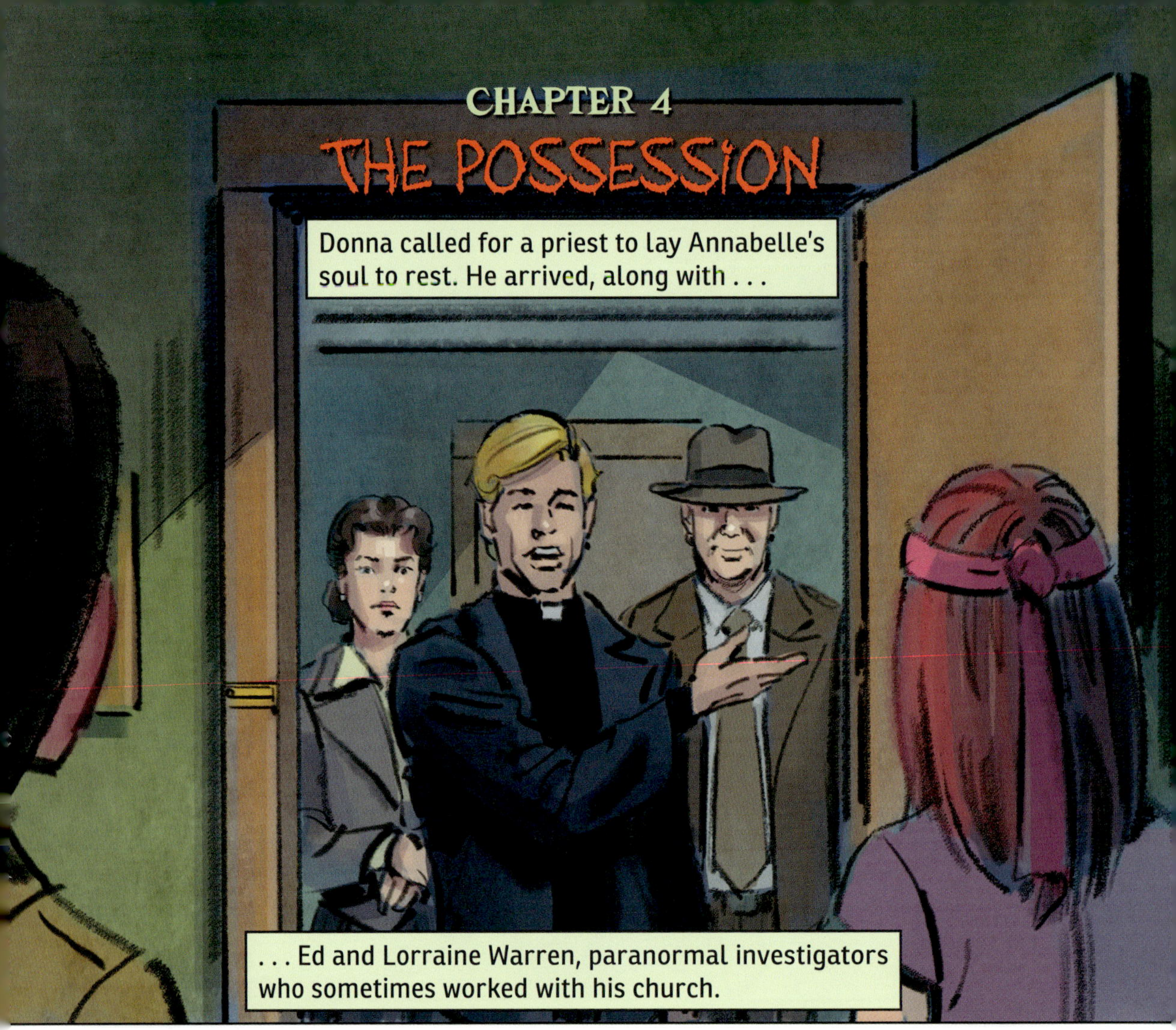
CHAPTER 4
THE POSSESSION
Donna called for a priest to lay Annabelle's soul to rest. He arrived, along with . . .
. . . Ed and Lorraine Warren, paranormal investigators who sometimes worked with his church.

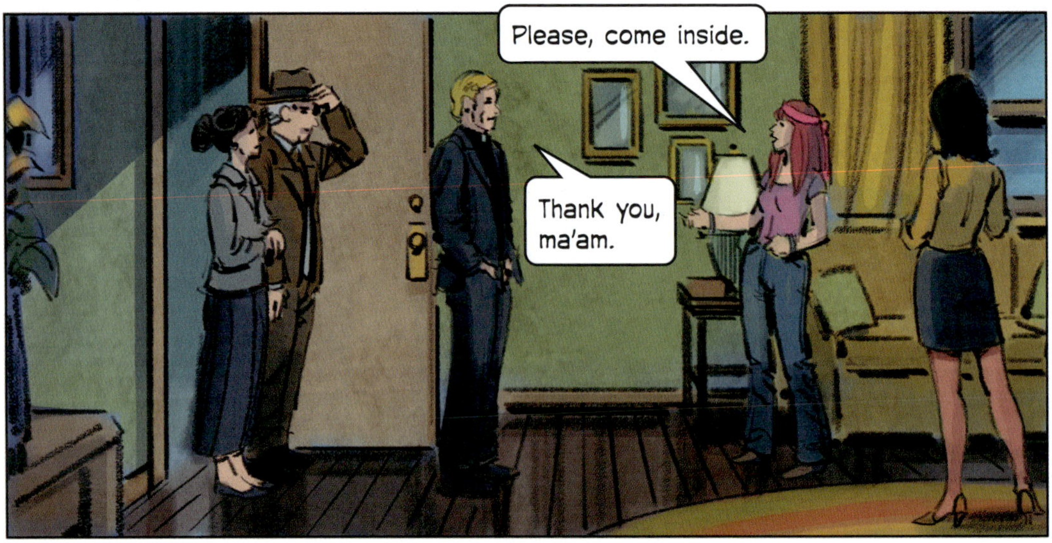
Please, come inside.
Thank you, ma'am.

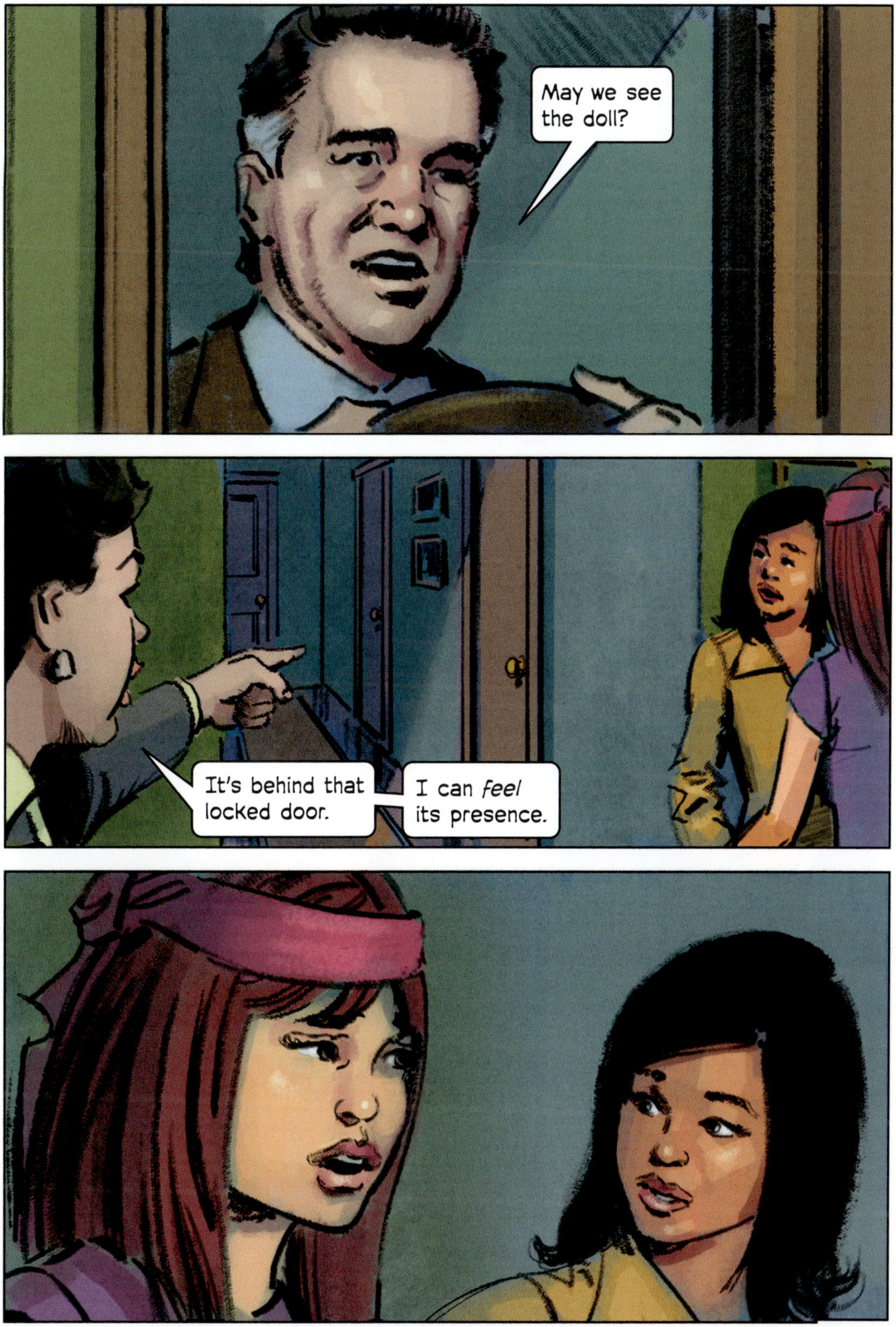
May we see the doll?
It's behind that locked door.
I can *feel* its presence.

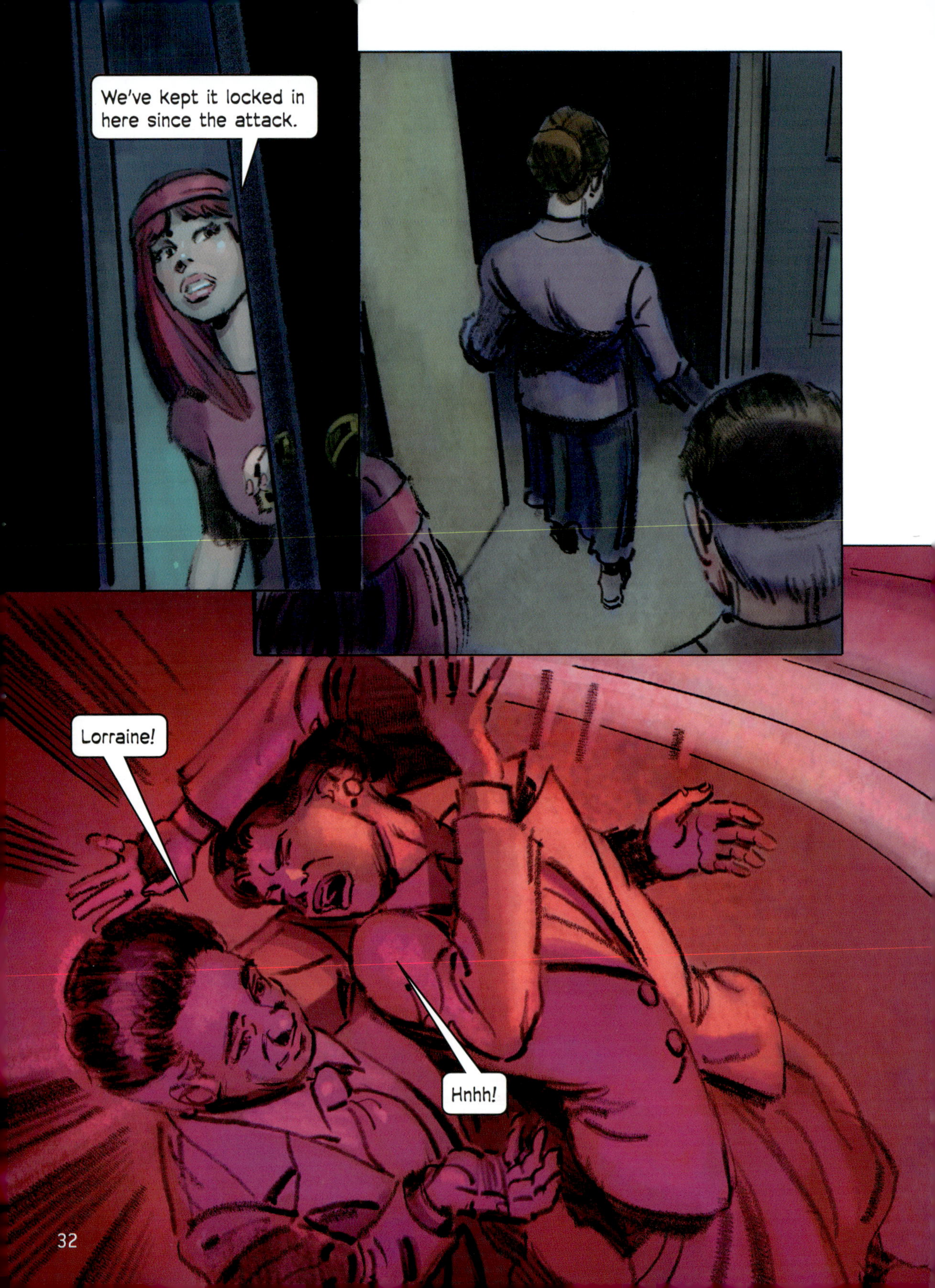
We've kept it locked in here since the attack.
Lorraine!
Hnhh!

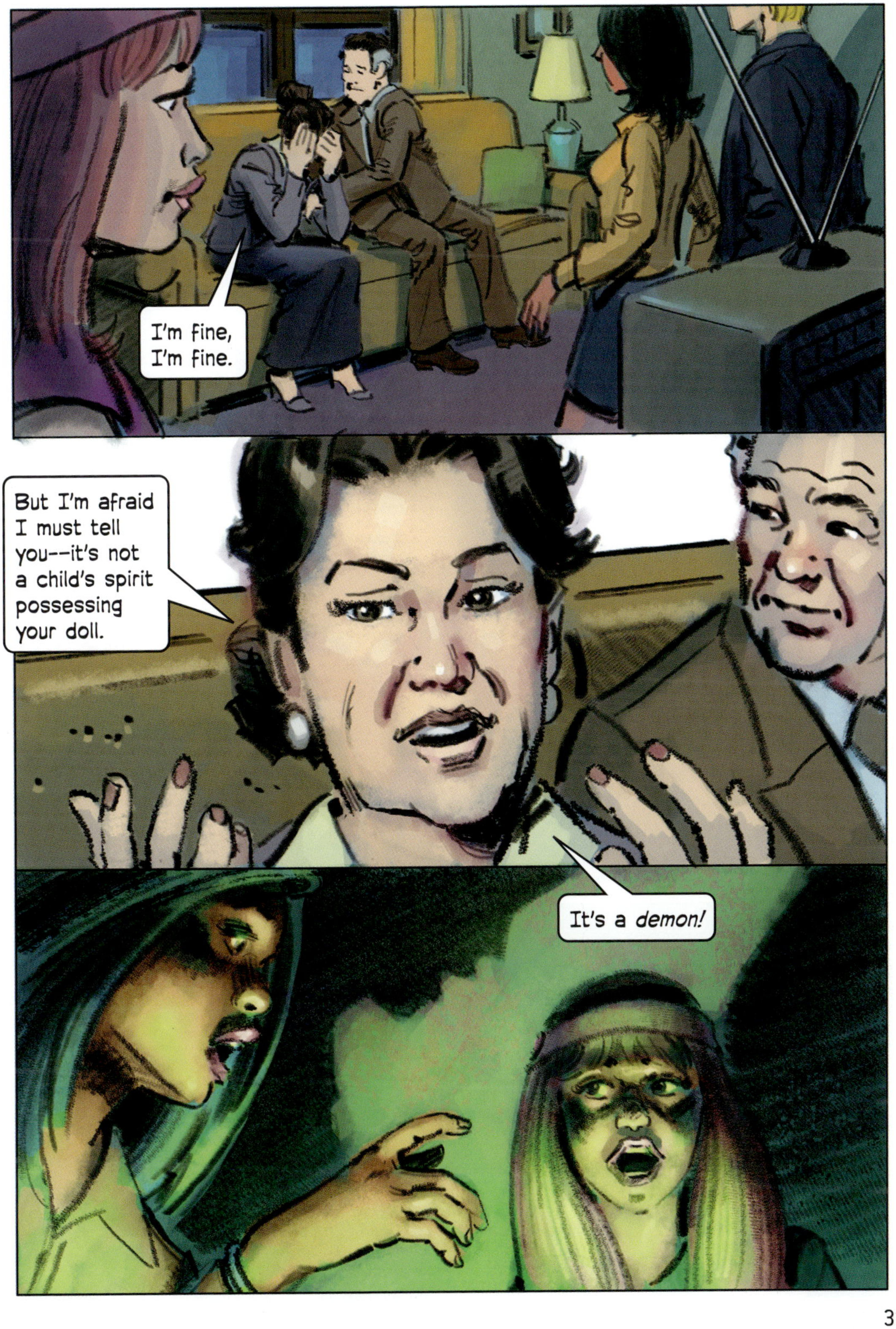
I'm fine, I'm fine.
But I'm afraid I must tell you--it's not a child's spirit possessing your doll.
It's a *demon!*

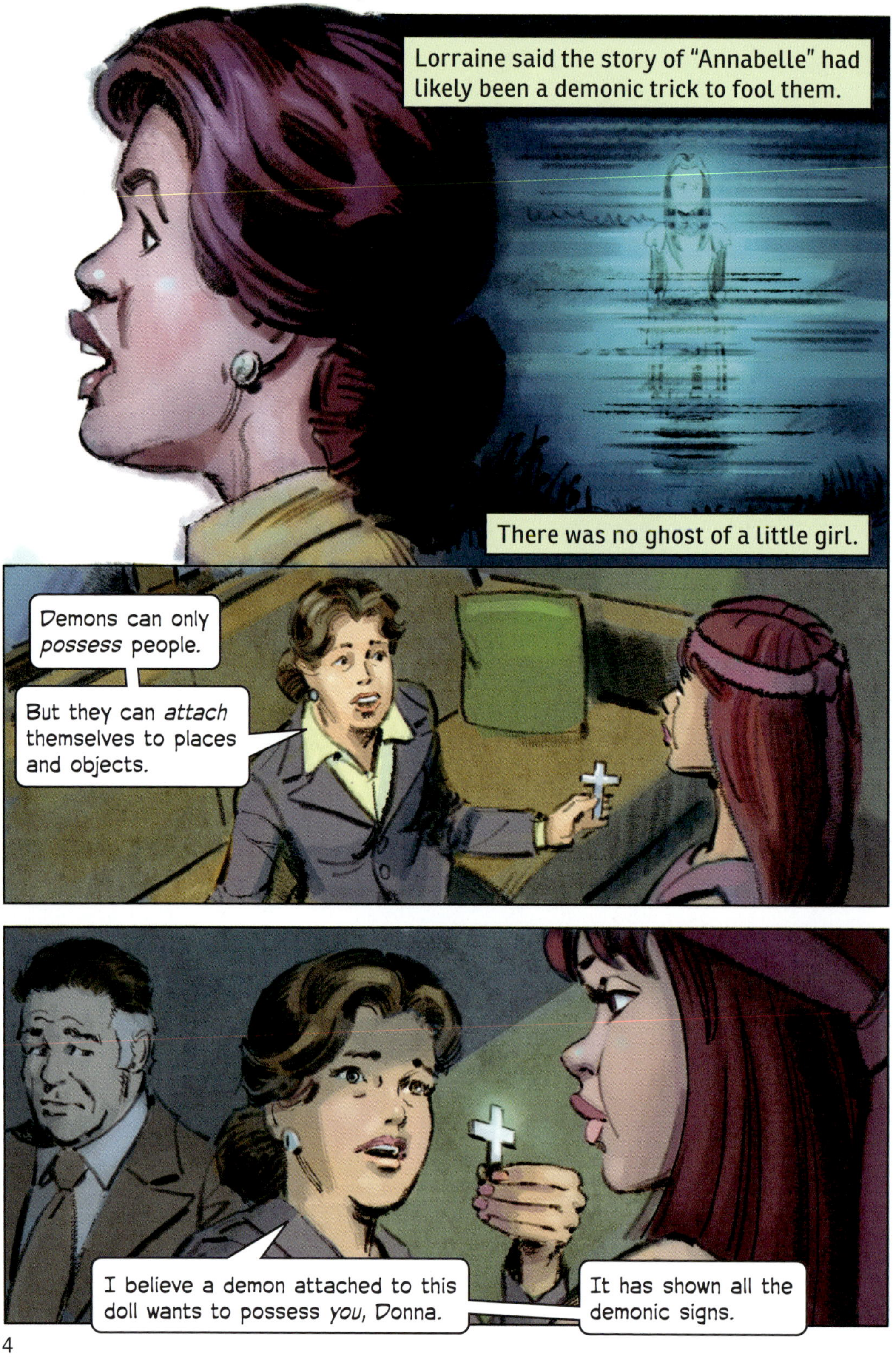

Lorraine said the story of "Annabelle" had likely been a demonic trick to fool them.
There was no ghost of a little girl.
Demons can only *possess* people.
But they can *attach* themselves to places and objects.
I believe a demon attached to this doll wants to possess *you*, Donna.
It has shown all the demonic signs.

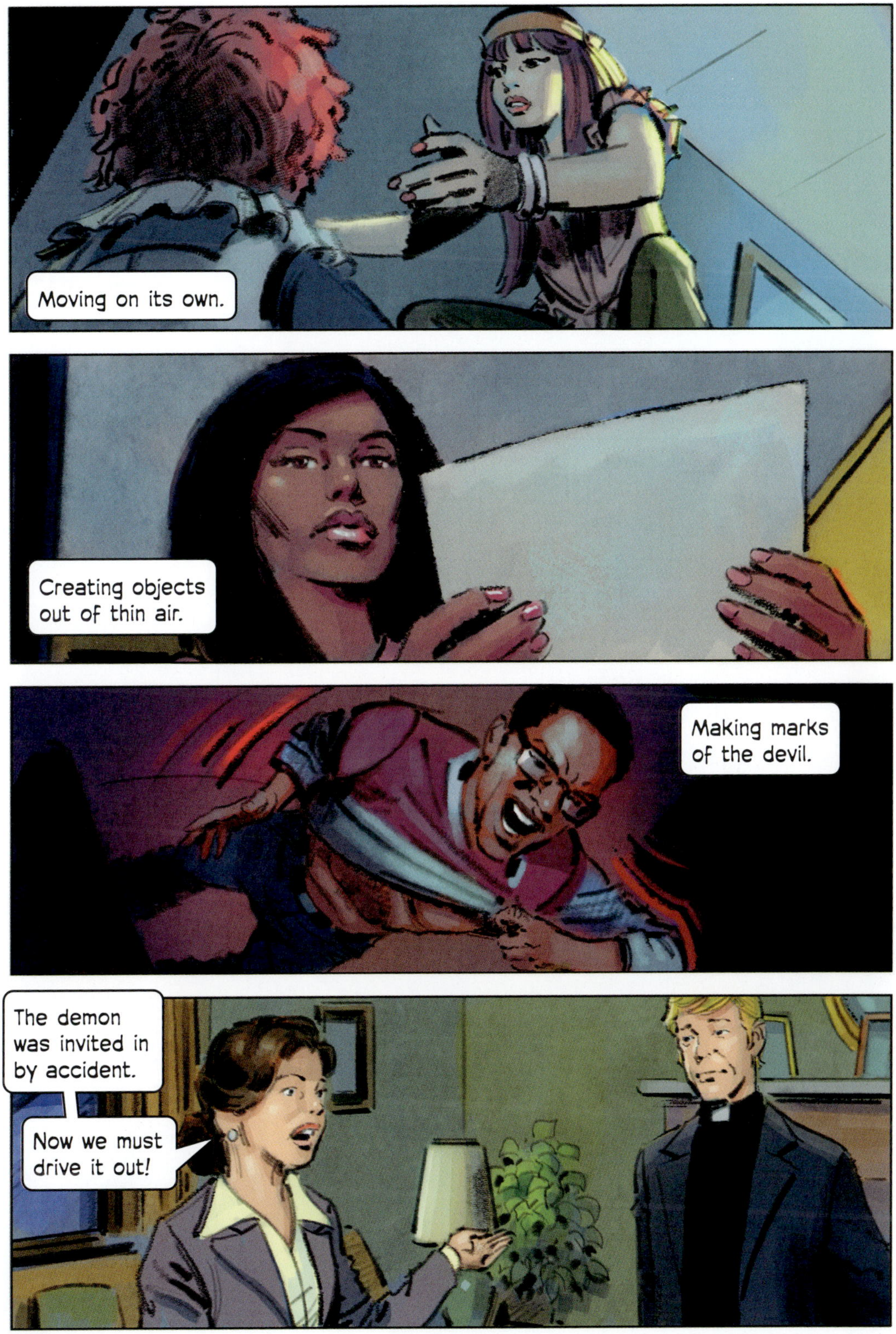
Moving on its own.
Creating objects out of thin air.
Making marks of the devil.
The demon was invited in by accident.
Now we must drive it out!

CHAPTER 5

THE FINAL RESTING PLACE

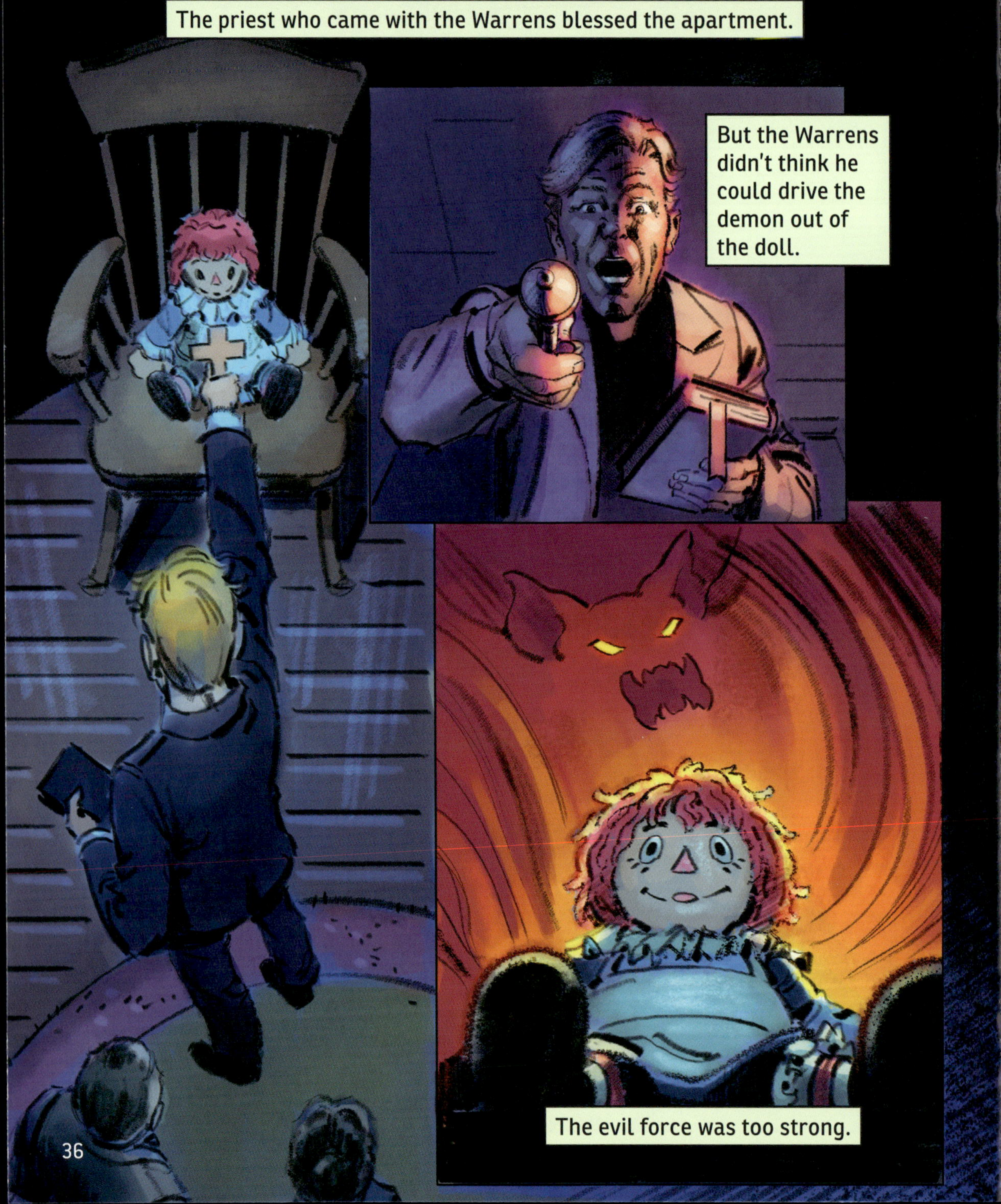

The priest who came with the Warrens blessed the apartment.
But the Warrens didn't think he could drive the demon out of the doll.
The evil force was too strong.

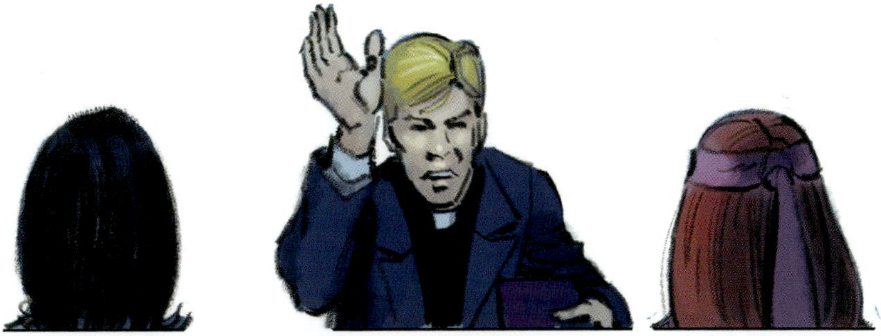

So the priest cleansed Donna, Angie, and their apartment.

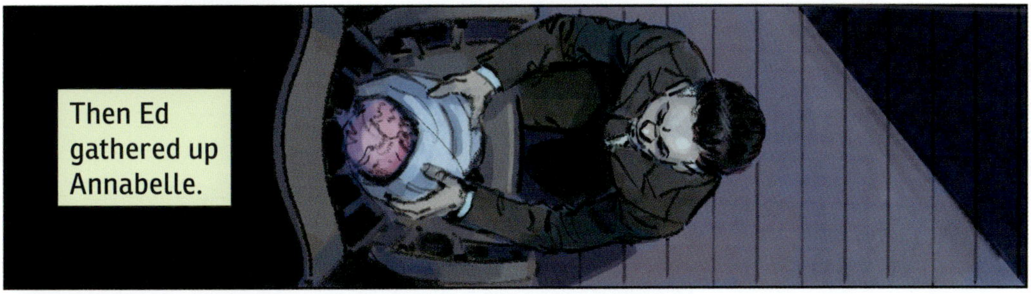
Then Ed gathered up Annabelle.

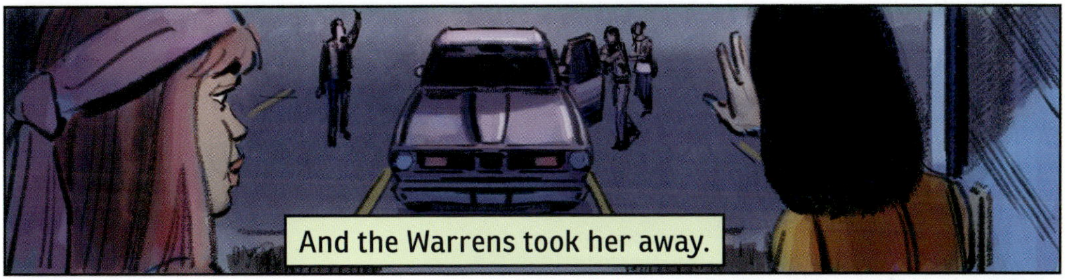
And the Warrens took her away.

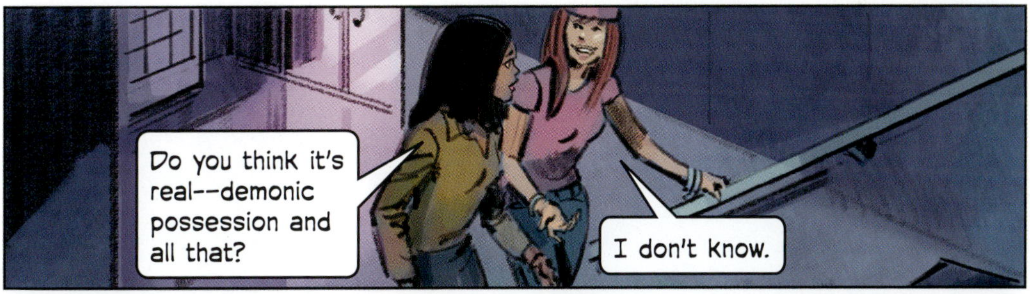
Do you think it's real--demonic possession and all that?
I don't know.

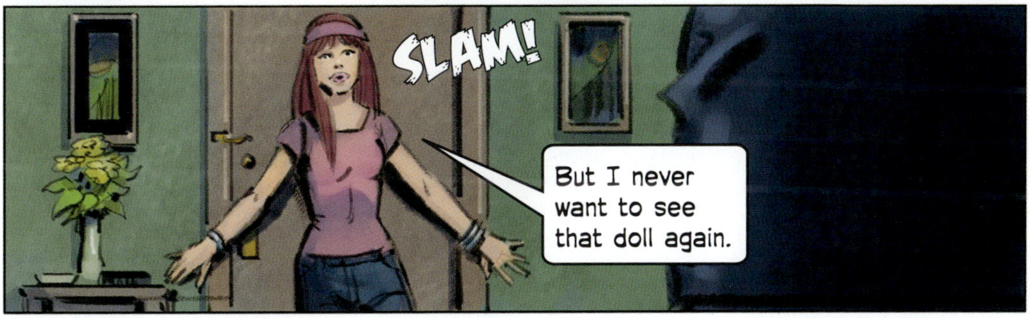
SLAM!
But I never want to see that doll again.

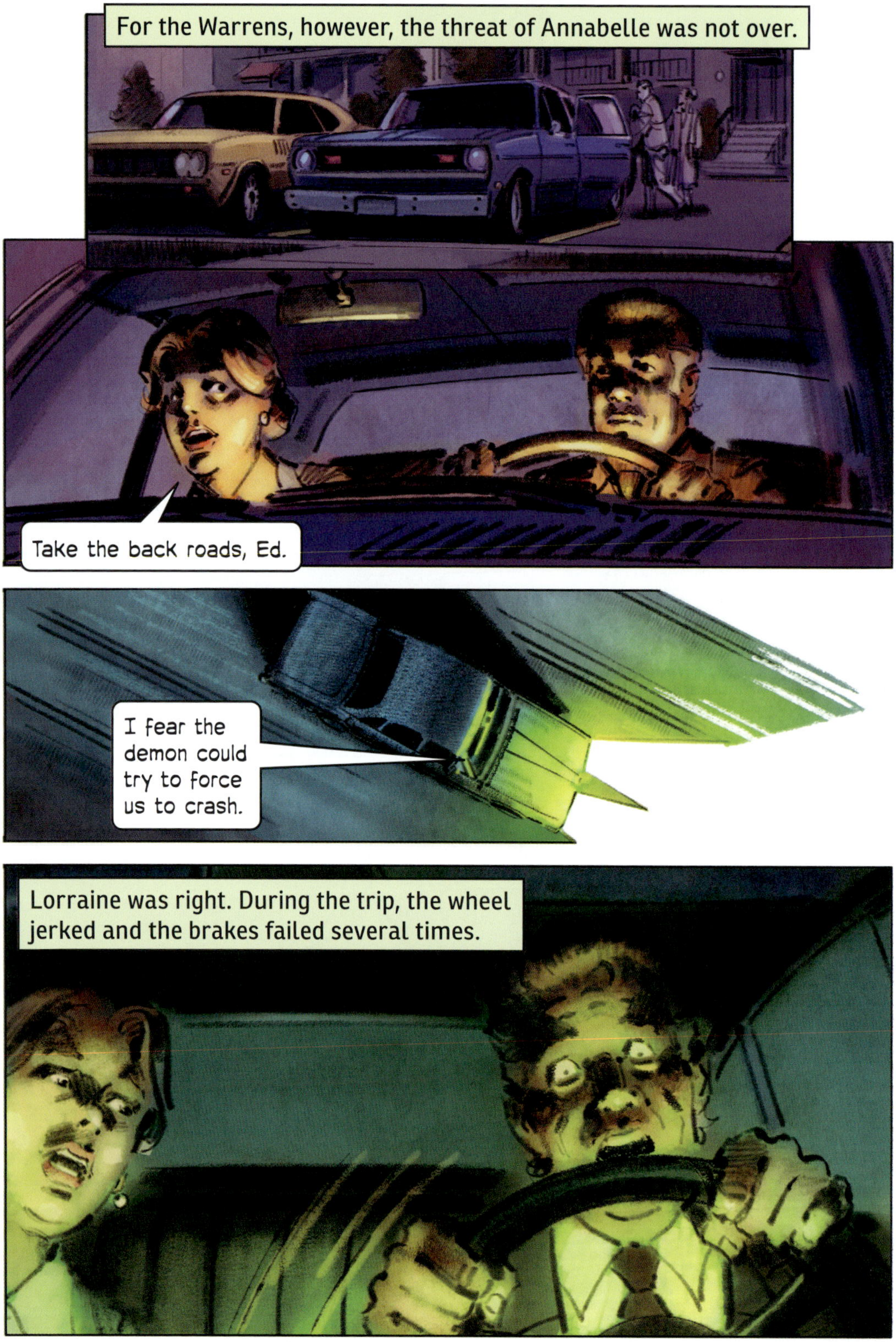
For the Warrens, however, the threat of Annabelle was not over.
Take the back roads, Ed.
I fear the demon could try to force us to crash.
Lorraine was right. During the trip, the wheel jerked and the brakes failed several times.

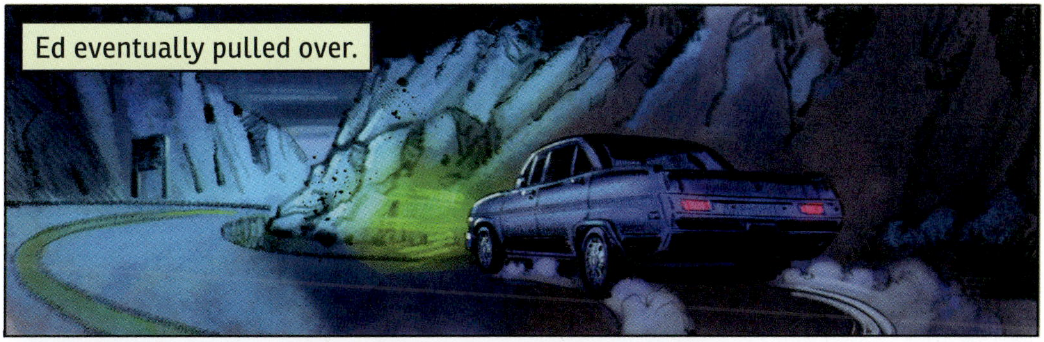
Ed eventually pulled over.

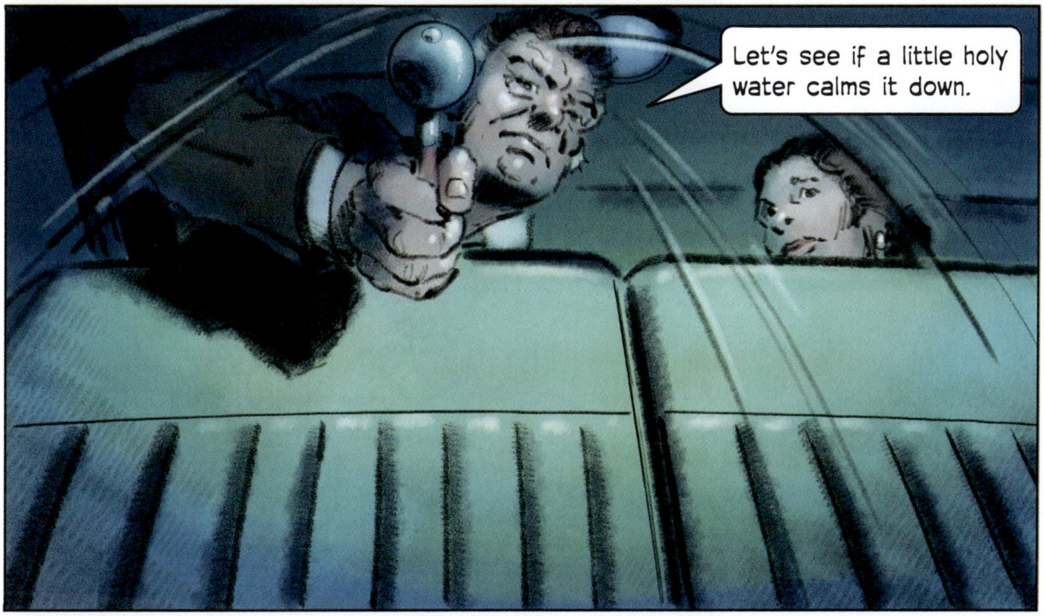
Let's see if a little holy water calms it down.

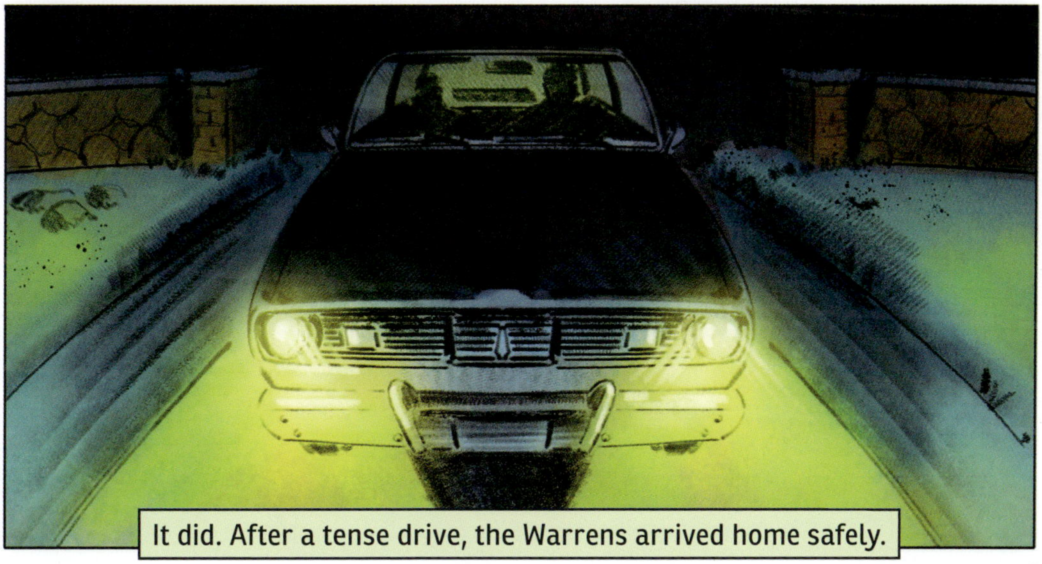
It did. After a tense drive, the Warrens arrived home safely.

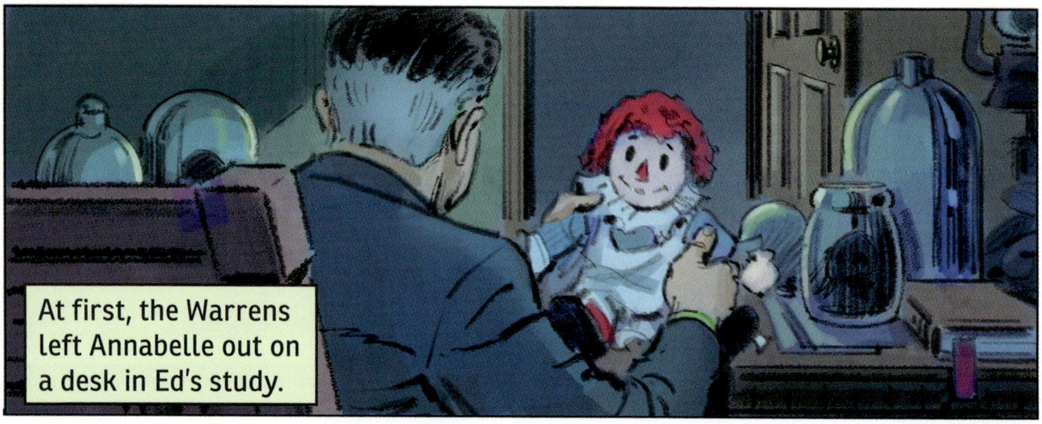
At first, the Warrens left Annabelle out on a desk in Ed's study.

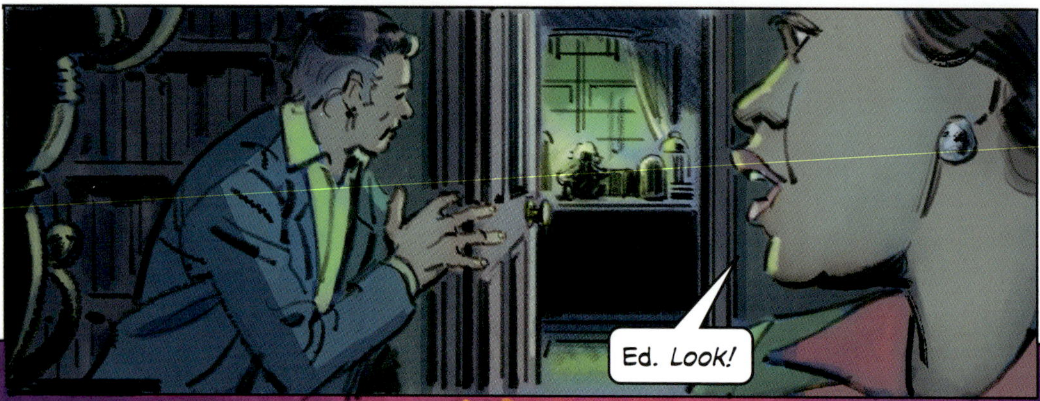
Ed. *Look!*

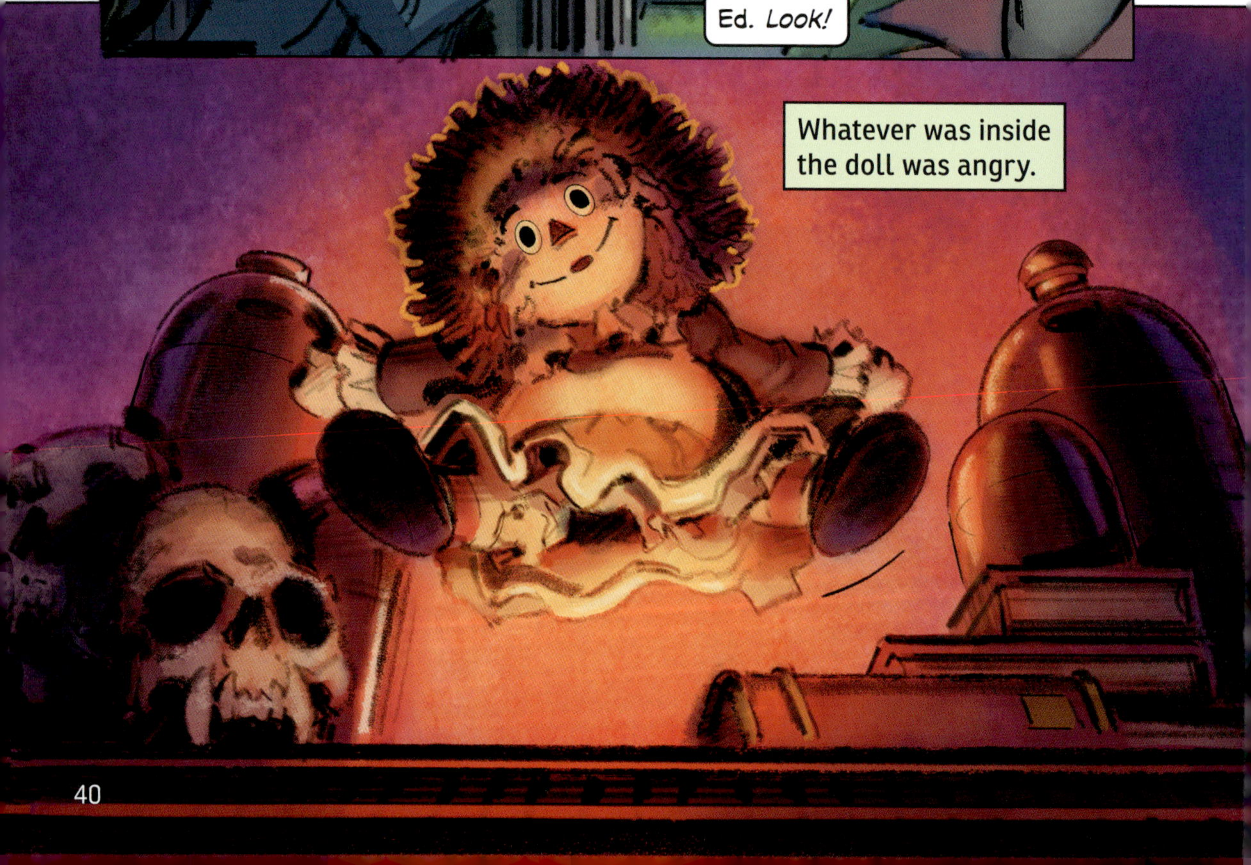
Whatever was inside the doll was angry.

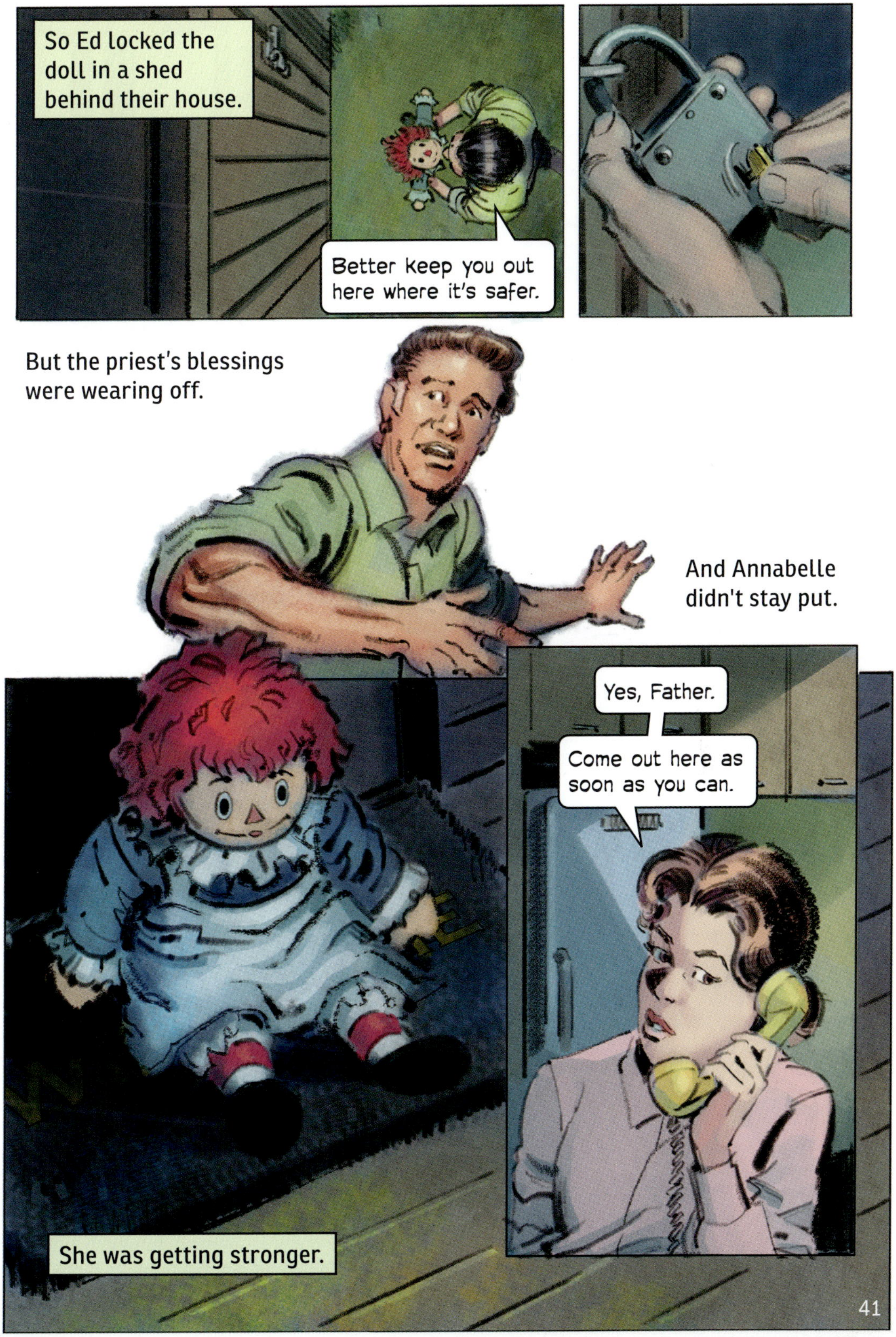
So Ed locked the doll in a shed behind their house.
Better keep you out here where it's safer.
But the priest's blessings were wearing off.
And Annabelle didn't stay put.
Yes, Father.
Come out here as soon as you can.
She was getting stronger.

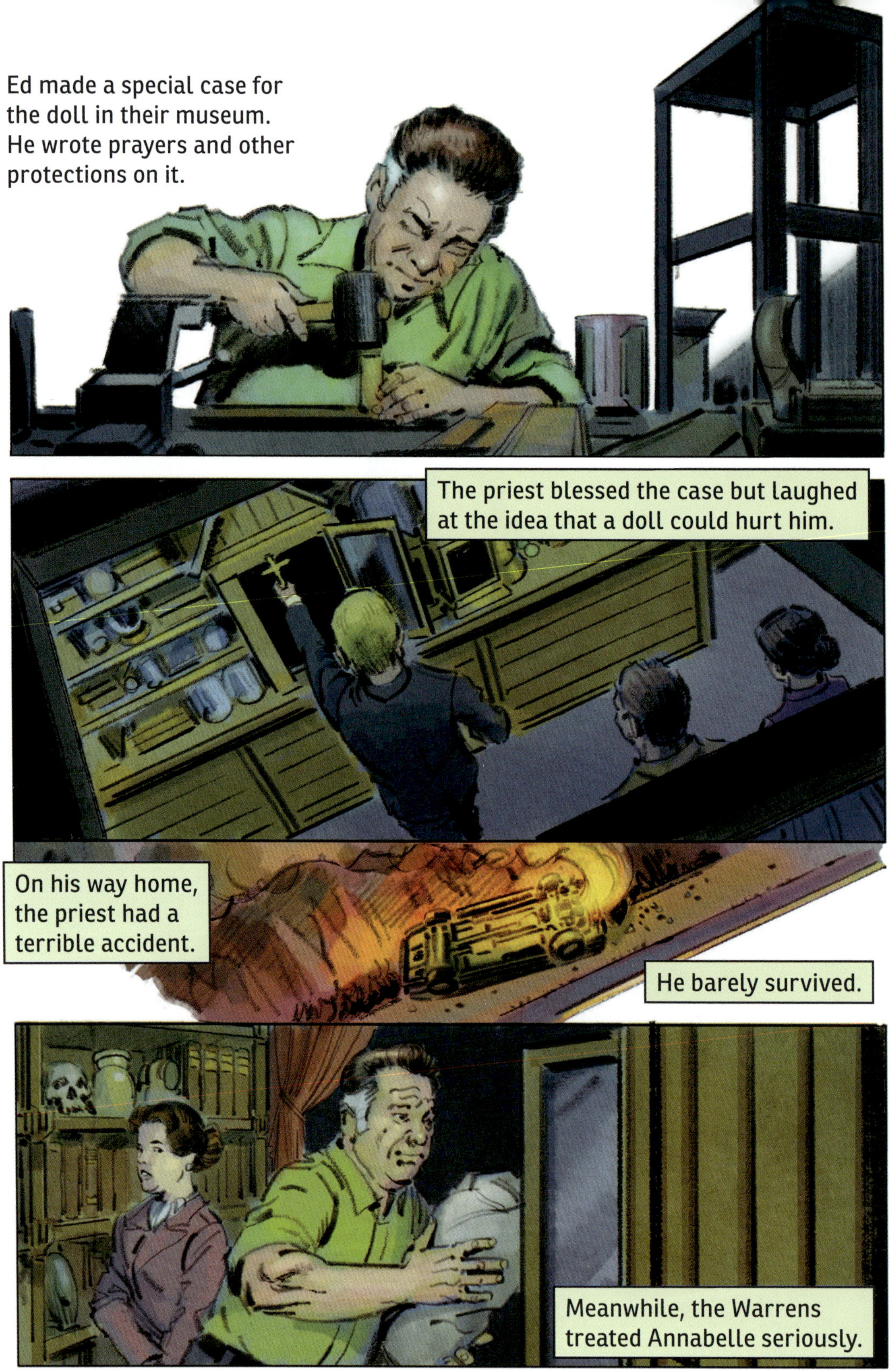
Ed made a special case for the doll in their museum. He wrote prayers and other protections on it.
The priest blessed the case but laughed at the idea that a doll could hurt him.
On his way home, the priest had a terrible accident.
He barely survived.
Meanwhile, the Warrens treated Annabelle seriously.

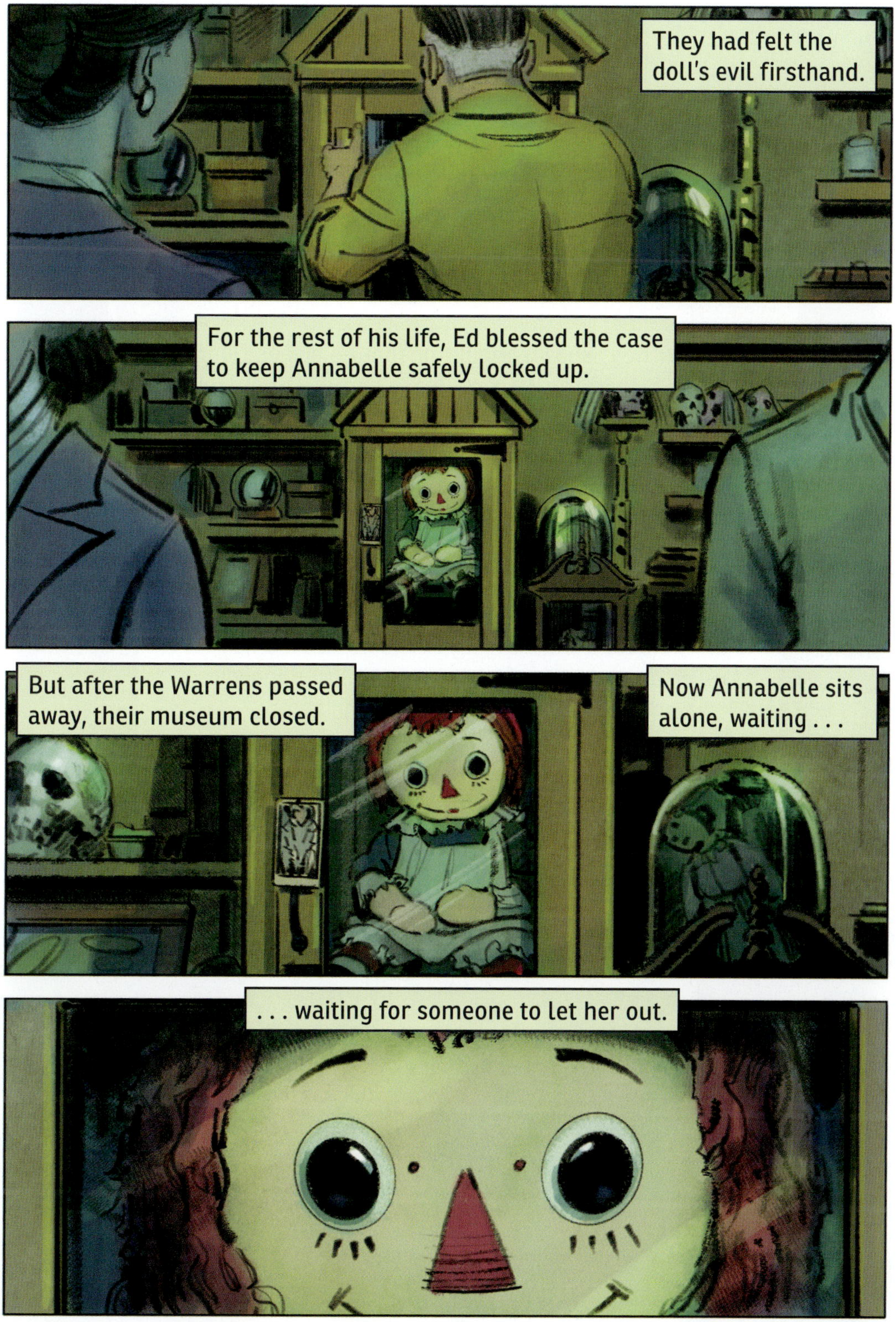
They had felt the doll's evil firsthand.
For the rest of his life, Ed blessed the case to keep Annabelle safely locked up.
But after the Warrens passed away, their museum closed.
Now Annabelle sits alone, waiting . . .
. . . waiting for someone to let her out.

More About Annabelle

- Very little is known about Annabelle's owner, Donna. Some believe the Warrens made her up. Others think her name was changed to protect her identity.

- Annabelle is a Raggedy Ann doll based on a character created in the early 1900s. Raggedy Ann has red yarn hair and a triangle nose.

- The Warrens founded the New England Society for Psychic Research in 1952. It is often said to be the oldest paranormal research organization in America.

- In 1975, the Warrens investigated the haunting of George and Kathy Lutz's house in Long Island, New York. The "haunting" is now believed to have been a hoax, but the case inspired the *Amityville Horror* book and movies.

- The Warrens' investigations have been adapted into *The Conjuring* and the *Annabelle* movies. The movies are loosely based on the "real" stories and treat the supernatural elements as fact, not fiction.

- Many experts believe the Warrens made up most of their reports. While the Warrens believed in the paranormal, they also made money on their cases. There is no proof they ever came across a "real" possession, haunting, ghost, or demon.

GLOSSARY

bless (BLESS)—to make sacred

cleanse (KLENZ)—to make something clean or pure

demon (DEE-muhn)—a devil or evil spirit

medium (MEE-dee-uhm)—a person who claims to make contact with spirits of the dead

paranormal (pair-uh-NOR-muhl)—having to do with an unexplained event that has no scientific explanation

possess (puh-ZESS)—to seize and take control of something

presence (PREZ-uhnss)—something, such as a spirit, that is felt and believed to be nearby

priest (PREEST)—a member of a church who leads church services and performs religious rites

spirit (SPEER-it)—a ghost

vessel (VESS-uhl)—a container

READ MORE

Fitzpatrick, Insha. *Chilling with Ghosts: A Totally Factual Field Guide to the Supernatural.* Philadelphia: Quirk Books, 2023.

Hoena, Blake. *The Deadly Bell Witch Ghost: A Ghostly Graphic.* North Mankato, MN: Capstone Press, 2024.

Katz, Susan B. *Haunted Dolls.* Minneapolis: Lerner Publications, 2023.

INTERNET SITES

CT Insider: Ed and Lorraine Warren: The History and the Investigations
ctpost.com/projects/2021/visuals/ed-lorraine-warren

Entertainment Weekly: The Conjuring: *The 'Real' Story in Pictures*
ew.com/gallery/conjuring-real-story-pictures

The Saturday Evening Post: Conjuring the Real Ed and Lorraine Warren
saturdayeveningpost.com/2019/10/conjuring-the-real-ed-and-lorraine-warren

ABOUT THE AUTHOR

Photo by Andrew Wolfe

Andrew Wolfe is the pseudonym of an author trying to avoid the wrath of unruly spirits. He haunts the chilly forests of the American Midwest, where he lives with his partner and dog. You can find his other work here and there, if you look hard enough.

ABOUT THE ILLUSTRATOR

Photo by Richter Studio

Jason Millet has provided illustration work for publishing, advertising, television, and films. His clients include NBC-Universal, Fox, Amblin Partners, HBO, Showtime, Disney, DC Comics, *The Wall Street Journal*, Scholastic Books, Wizards of the Coast, and Dark Horse Publishing among many others. Additionally, he has worked on ad campaigns for everything from Ford trucks to Happy Meals. He lives in Chicago with his wife, daughter, and very scary house cat.